DANCE TO THE 7 TUNES OF SUCCESS

DANCE TO THE 7 TUNES OF SUCCESS

Change the world with your standards of excellence

NISHIT LAL

JAICO PUBLISHING HOUSE
Ahmedabad Bangalore Bhopal Bhubaneswar Chennai
Delhi Hyderabad Kolkata Lucknow Mumbai

Published by Jaico Publishing House
A-2 Jash Chambers, 7-A Sir Phirozshah Mehta Road
Fort, Mumbai - 400 001
jaicopub@jaicobooks.com
www.jaicobooks.com

DANCE TO THE 7 TUNES OF SUCCESS
ISBN 97978-81-8495-570-5

First Jaico Impression: 2014

Printed by
Rashmi Graphics
#3, Amrutwel CHS Ltd., C.S. #50/74
Ganesh Galli, Lalbaug, Mumbai - 400 012
E-mail: tiwarijp@vsnl.net

This is for you Mom, Dad and my dear sis Kiku

Table of Contents

Preface

Massive amounts of literature have been written on Success, yet the hunger of principles on success is still not satiated. People from different walks of life are seeking principles that can help them make instant changes in their lives. They are not looking for advice on Successful living because they know what to do; instead they are looking for easy to implement ideas on gaining strength, to follow through on what they know. This book gives you wealth of thoughts on expanding your personal power.

Everyone knows in which direction they must go; their heart knows it. The intuition gives them the direction, but it is the mind that must give power to move towards the right direction. You can never be happy if your heart is not into what you are doing at any given moment. Ignore the heart and you ignore your happiness, and when you listen to your heart, you are living your dream life. Today, we need strength to follow our dreams, passion to create energy every Monday and potential to follow through on our dreams – this book will remind you of the power you have.

But in today's fast-paced world, everyone would like to have "ready to use", "how to" strategies that help them achieve results they want in the minimum amount of time. This book provides a series of well-researched and usable ideas on taking your life to the next level. This book is all the more relevant to the ones who are living an awesomely beautiful life, because continuous life improvement is the law of nature. And for the ones who are still looking out for the answers, this may be the book which will get the reader started on the path of personal mastery. This book is not a book of knowledge but it's a book of small bite-sized thoughts which will excite you to move in a completely new direction in your life.

After having researched hundreds of books on personal development and success, I have found a common thread to personal power, which can be placed in seven domains of our lives – Passion, Productivity, Purpose, Perception, Possibilities, Practice and Potential. I firmly believe that to make changes in one's life, one must have a driving force which creates the momentum for a change – this driving force is called *Passion.* Ignite your passion and you are on the road to success. This chapter provides you with powerful ideas to explore your potential and to do a reality check of where you are and where you want to go.

When you know where you want to go and what you want to have in your life, it means that you have clarity of thought. Life is no more "I don't know where I am going"; instead it is "I have a *lakshya* (goal)". Many times I ask people what they want, they have an answer to it, but then I ask them "why" do they want what they want? They get confused. Hence you must define a purpose, which is a big "why" of your destination. Why you want to achieve what you want to achieve? *Purpose* gives you concrete ideas on knowing what you are here to do? Are you born an artist or an engineer, a painter or a salesman/woman?! Explore yourself with *Purpose.*

Once you have the *Passion* and the *Purpose* set right, you must take action and produce. Produce good ideas, creative thoughts and most importantly produce actions necessary by stepping forward and taking the first leap towards your journey of self-mastery. *Productivity* throws light on how you can fasten the process of self-development by getting a coach and better planning.

When you take action, you are bound to fail, and to see the failure as an opportunity, one must be ready to acquire the right *Perception.* It changes reality, taking clues from successful people and stories and gives you the message that one must see realities as they are and not worse than they are. The book goes further to share that even in the darkest times, the *Possibilities* life has to offer are endless. One must be willing to ask, seek and knock consistently to create opportunities if there aren't any. Through *Possibilities*, you will bear creative ideas, on how to tackle daily life problems that come your way by accepting the problem and then resolving it, instead of resisting it. Life doesn't get better just by taking action, but it gets better by consistently taking the right action. *Practice* gives out a plethora of ideas on how persistence, effective decisions and practice can make you close the gap of where you are and where you want to reach. At last, the goal of life should not be to collect materialistic possessions, but to realize our Potential and make a ding in the universe. In the chapter *Potential*, you will get to know that it's the person's will which can take him to heights of his potential, and that Faith is more important than reasons. Once you live by the faith of making it happen, it will happen. Faith moves the world.

When pieces of a jigsaw puzzle are joined together, we see the picture clearly. Similarly pieces of wisdom when joined together, in the right sequence and way, can make you see the pathway to the greatest treasure of life – your inner self. This is what the book is all about – "the way to Personal mastery". Enjoy reading it!

Best Wishes,
Nishit Lal

CHAPTER 1

Passion

One question that has always intrigued me throughout my life is "What makes people different?" In searching for the answer, I have realized that it is energy that makes all the difference. Life is really all about energy management. How much of your energy do you give around you – to your relationship, at your workplace, at home or on the playground? High-octane people do more, listen more, act more, think more, study more and feel more. Their presence is electric and overwhelming and it is this that differentiates people who move up in life from those who give up. Some call it magnetism, others call it charisma. You can give it many flowery adjectives, but the fact is that charismatic people do make a difference wherever they go.

Haven't you seen people who dynamize the atmosphere with their infectious presence? They create massive amounts of emotional energy in people, enough for them to achieve a goal or change their lifestyle. You possess this appeal that is in you like a dormant trait and which can spread like wildfire, no matter where you go.

Ever wondered how? Live your passion and your attraction will soar. The source of charisma lies in passion. People who can tap into the source of their passion become charismatic. They are easily spotted. The way they look, speak and walk is remarkably different from those who have not yet realized their potential. These people tend to explore and exploit their talent with greater success than others.

Just as success has its roots in hard work, charisma has its roots in passion. Passion can give you the energy to influence people. It can provide you the leverage to rise above others. Passion can show you what you are made of. We say, "You can't judge a book by its cover". Similarly, you can't judge a person by his appearance; you need to look for his passion.

There have been great debates on how to detect your passion and there have been no final answers; we await the resolution of an issue that philosophers have been debating for ages.

Inevitably, there have been many debates on how to discover your passion and there have been no conclusive answers. Philosophers say, "Life is not about finding yourself, it is about creating yourself." While they continue with their quest and debate, we await the resolution ceaselessly. So a question worth asking yourself is how to find your passion. The answer is you can't find your passion, either you create it or you let it find you. What I have indeed realized is that you must let passion seek you and not the other way round. However, finding your passion is not the final objective; rather it is only the jumpstart to a more meaningful life.

As T S Eliot has rightly said, "We begin on a journey, and having journeyed afar we return to the place we began, only to know it for the first time".

Have your own standards of excellence

All your efforts will help you find your true self; there is nothing outside that you need to find. It's all within. Your passion lies within.

The Fire Within

Success is not the result of spontaneous combustion.
You must first set yourself on fire.

–Fred Shero

People often ask, "What is passion, where can I see it and what does it look like?"

A good way to study passion is to read about and know people who are truly passionate in their lives. It is about understanding their worldview, their focus and their beliefs. People become passionate when they do what they love; they spend hours doing what they love without feeling tired or bored. Each day of their lives is full of the fun and enthusiasm of doing something new and challenging. Their energy is infectious.

They're ready to take risks and utilize opportunities. They do not do it to acquire a salary hike or a promotion or a trip abroad, but to attain contentment beyond measure, for themselves.

An ordinary person works to sustain himself or to achieve the result his employer expects, but passionate people work beyond these expectations, they go beyond job descriptions, they do the uncalled for. They devise their own standards of excellence. Excellence, for them, is fulfilling the task at hand; they work towards stretching themselves beyond their sphere and raising their standard.

- Michael Jordan didn't play basketball with the intention of a promotion or a salary hike. He stuck with his vocation during tough times, did his best and later reaped the benefits of his passion.
- JK Rowling continued writing in a café as a divorced, unemployed mother when she could not

afford to support herself and her daughter. She kept going even when publishers repeatedly rejected her manuscript. She found inspiration in her books, which transformed the course of her life.

- Henry Ford had a couple of failed business attempts before he founded the Ford Motor Company which changed the automobile market worldwide. He saw challenges and opportunities where other people saw failures.

When we say, one cigarette reduces the life of a person by an hour; not following your passion reduces it by days.

When you enjoy any productive activity which is of considerable value to others, time flies. Maybe David Beckham feels as if he has just begun even after having trained on the field for hours! You lose track of time when you work on something you love doing.

Positive psychologist Mihály Csíkszentmihályi calls this stage a 'flow' in performance, when a person loses track of time while doing something. People from all walks of life experience a state of flow, when they are consciously and completely immersed in an activity.

Other phrases are also employed to define this state such as being 'in the flow', 'in the zone', 'in the groove', 'on fire' and so on. You experience 'flow' in activities you love doing.

How will your passion find you? Sometimes you simply stumble upon your passion and realize what you are meant to do your whole life! Everything starts with that moment of love. In the moment of love, your creative juices are released.

To allow your passion to find you, take up various projects and assignments. Variety is the spice of life and so if you need that spice to juice up your life, you must be open to changes that come your way. If you are working, go beyond your job description and do something new; if you are a student, go beyond your academic curriculum and indulge in your hobbies; if you are a businessman, take the risk of venturing into an unexplored business avenue and engage with your interest. You never know the power of experience. The more experience you have, the more aware you are of yourself. That brings us to the question…

Do you have to start early to kindle the fire of passion? The answer is no. Passion knows no age. Fauja Singh, a man who is passionate about running marathons, is one such example. He broke many records during his heyday. Little did people know that he is a centenarian! He has a passion for running and he wants to run till his last breath. It doesn't matter whether you are 18 or 81 – you can light a fire anytime, anywhere. Singh definitely lives up to the adage that age is just a number!

Explore the World

We shall not cease from exploration, and the end of all our exploring will be to arrive where we started and know the place for the first time.

–TS Eliot

When, in the days of yore, the boat had been invented, people thought it was dangerous to go beyond the safety of the shores. There were mythic tales warning people against losing sight of land. People were scared of treading beyond the boundaries that were set by sailors. But one day, a sailor decided to sail beyond the borders, which metaphorically implies a fear of the unknown. He crossed a gigantic sea and its wrath and finally discovered the land that later came to be known as America. This sailor – the Great Admiral who left his mark on the world map and changed the course of history was none other than Christopher Columbus.

This story is nothing but a metaphor for us to know that only when we go beyond the imaginary lines we have drawn for ourselves can we create a better future for ourselves and for everyone around us. Boats, like human beings, are not meant to stay within their limits.

The greatest regret a man can ever have is to recognize that the only limits set on his potential are internal. All limitations are those of an exhausted human mind that are meant to be broken, transcended or replaced. The purpose of human life is to grow because stagnation is equal to death. However, for growth to materialize, there should be a consistent pursuit to raise the bar, extend limits and create new and broader horizons...

Once upon a time, there were three guitars kept in a store. The owner took one guitar and stretched the wire, and it was very painful. On seeing the guitar in pain, one guitar hid behind the shelf while the other did not show any fear. So the owner took the second guitar and stretched it too. But the third guitar was behind the shelf so it was saved. After a month, a world famous guitarist came to buy the guitars from the owner. The guitarist showed him all the three guitars. On playing the guitars he noticed that two guitars which were stretched, played very well and struck the right note while the third didn't. So he went on to buy the two. In life too, people will admire you, love you when you will be of value to them, which will happen when you stretch yourself beyond your current potential. You must go beyond what you are doing to find your passion; you must be open to new roles, new professions and new engagements until you stumble on the path that is designed for your life.

Harrison Ford, the eminent Hollywood actor who has starred in numerous blockbusters, was a carpenter before he became a movie star. Many people may not be aware of how the celebrated basketball player, Michael Jordan, switched from one career to another. He started his career in basketball, announced an early retirement and began a second career in baseball. He soon retired from that too, only to play a few more seasons of basketball. Today, he is known as a legendary basketball player and one of the most effectively marketed stars in the sports industry.

All these people explored numerous options in their career to find their true purpose. There is only one formula which will give you an edge in life – and that is to continuously explore your potential.

Sometimes it may feel like exploring in the dark, but I will suggest you keep shooting until you hit the target. You may have several misses while doing this, you may feel dejected, but only after these failures will you know where not to hit.

I too found my true calling this way. I pursued engineering because of peer pressure. After four years, I realized that it was not the right place for me. I had to do something beyond engineering. So I joined the Information Technology industry, expecting I would truly be satisfied. But not for long; I soon realized that this was not the right place for me and decided to move on.

While I was trying to discover my area of interest, I had realized that analytics was not one my strong points, I did not enjoy developing software, and neither was I interested in engineering. Hereafter, I took a step that I believed was the right one, and enrolled in a course on Human Resources. And it was at this time that I discovered a passion that I would commit my life to – helping people live better. It took me eight years to reach this stage of self-awareness, of knowing what I am here for. Conducting training programs, writing books and counseling people to enable them live a joyful life – that's my purpose.

The task is to keep exploring and experimenting because everyone is here to do special things in special ways. Bill Gates was to revolutionize the computer industry; Sam Walton was to master supply chain management; Mother Teresa was here to help save the lives of millions with her compassion for the underprivileged; Steven Spielberg was meant to direct world class blockbuster movies and Peter Drucker was here to develop revolutionary management theories.

Finding your purpose may involve exploring several options before settling down to one. Every moment you see new avenues in front of themselves, old doors closing and paths changing, your effort should be towards moving forward and learning from the past.

I have met many retired people who say that they regret not having trusted their instincts. They chose a secure career, they married because they were conformists, and they killed their dreams to fulfill the whims and fancies of their families. They lived the lives others wanted them to live and in the process lost their own sense of identity.

Ask yourself:

What am I special at? Remember what you were good at when you were a child. What talents have you acquired with age? How many options have you evaluated in your career? Think how you could bring in a change and do something different. Have you gone beyond the job assigned to you, and if you have, was it enjoyable? Have you discovered any hobbies or interests beyond your routine tasks? Awareness brings results. Know more about yourself than what you have known in the past.

Live Your Dreams

> *I'm a dreamer. I have to dream and reach for the stars, and if I miss a star then I grab a handful of clouds.*
>
> –Mike Tyson

Do you have a dream life?

If the answer to this question is yes, then it is phenomenal, but if your answer is no, then why not, I ask you. It is our birthright to create and draw on the abundance available to everyone we know yet we make little effort in choosing what we want and refusing what we don't want. Life is all about choosing items from a catalogue. But one needs to pick up the catalogue in the first place. It all boils down to choosing and deciding.

Dreams work only when you begin to work

We do this by drawing a picture of what we want in our minds. Arnold Schwarzenegger had a dream of becoming a world class body builder and he achieved it. He didn't stop there. He dreamed of making it big in Hollywood and worked hard to fulfill his dreams. Martin Luther King Jr. too 'had a dream' – his dreams were of a nation of racial equality, brotherhood, freedom and justice. And with his dream he brought about a revolution which changed the world. Dreams work only when you begin to work.

Knowing your dream is as important as breathing. It keeps you alive, motivated and passionate. The vitality of your dream is reflected in the way you walk and talk. Your dream can change the way you feel about yourself.

I often hear people say they do not know what they want. What I suggest is even if you don't know what you want, you can ask yourself the counter question, what it is that you do not want. Sometimes knowing what you don't want can give you the answer. I recently went to an ice cream parlor to have some dessert after my dinner. When I entered the parlor, I didn't know what I wanted so I looked at the menu. There were around 15 types of ice creams and sundaes available. I started to eliminate my options on the basis of what I knew I didn't like. I didn't like cola cream sundae, I didn't like pineapple ice cream, and I didn't particularly enjoy rum n' raisins. I finally came down to three options. So I chose from amongst the three and took the ice cream that seemed to be the most appealing.

Make a list of all the dreams you want to accomplish in this lifetime. Be as weird as possible. The weirder the dream, the more motivated you will feel about it.

Someone once said that it is not the reasonable man who changed the world, but the unreasonable man who makes changes – the ones who dream up the impossible and then work to realize them.

Knowing your dream and living it are two completely different things. People may know their dreams but only a fraction of them live it. Knowing your dream only in your head is like seeing the invisible. Most of the time people are not aware of their dreams and that is why they live haphazard lives, moving hither and thither aimlessly. Awareness of your dreams can direct you towards the path you want in life. To materialize your dream, you need resources, people and emotions.

You must have resources to accomplish your dream. Ask yourself what skills you might require to achieve your dreams. A consistent search of your key resources – knowledge, social and emotional resources – will assist you in the pursuit of your dream. Listing the resources you need will help you develop your master plan.

You can't achieve everything on your own. Question yourself. Can anyone help me achieve my dream? Does anyone have a similar accomplishment? How did they do it? How much human capital would I need to get my project underway? Will my friends assist me? People are there to help you out but you need to share your dream with them. With asking begins receiving.

Emotions have power, utilize this power. Knowing why you have a particular dream will make all the difference when it comes to achieving it. Your motivation will be determined by the reason behind your dream. Happiness, love, joy, excitement and passion are the most powerful emotions felt by a human being. Your dream, if fueled by these emotions, can launch you in a big way and give you all the motivation you need to act upon your dream.

We have zillions of desires that we wish would materialize. Yet almost always, we play small and never try to venture beyond what we have. This fear stops us from fulfilling ourselves. We spend time realizing someone else's dream instead of working on our own. Either live your life or someone else's – the choice is yours.

Quality Work

Quality is not an act, it is a habit.

–Aristotle

Would you like to go to a restaurant where the food is stale? Or would you like to fly in a plane that offers all of the world's luxury but for a few loose nuts on the wing?! You would never like to take such kinds of risks, would you? In our daily dealings, we sometimes forget and take short cuts in our work, which reduce the quality of our products and services. In the corporate world, billions are spent just to ensure the services are of high quality. Ever thought why? It is because in this day and age, the war of the corporate world is not won on the basis of the number of products and services that have been offered; rather the game is all about the quality of products and services that reach the customer.

Your work should speak of your commitment to quality every time it reaches the user. Start with the small tasks you do daily and give them your best. You should be on schedule and the finished product should look phenomenal. Superior quality cars are not just about the decor; rather its engine is as important as its décor that many of us fail to realize. After all, what is the point of having a Formula 1 car with a poor-quality engine? Focusing on the quality of individual parts ensures the quality of the product in its entirety. All your tasks, no matter how small, should similarly speak of your caliber. Combined with other parts, the whole will proclaim your merit.

Compose your own life and your own work

Many people in their pursuit of quality begin to spend endless hours at their work. They believe the more time they spend, the better their product will be. What we need to know is that it isn't the quantity but quality of time which makes the mark. At workplace too, many relate the number of hours put in by an employee to his performance but what we need to examine is what he has put in during the scheduled office time. Generating more value with minimal resources is a sign of quality.

Do your work like there's no tomorrow. If you are preparing for an examination or developing a product, mark it with your signature of quality. The Japanese word *kaizen*, which means change for the best or continuous improvement, can be integrated into your own life and at every stage.

It is just like running a 100-meter race – the first time you run the distance in 20 seconds, you feel happy. Now you set your resolve harder, use *kaizen*, and find out ways to reduce this time by 4 seconds. Find solutions and implement them. In this way, at every step you strive for continuous improvement. That's how a sprinter breaks world records. The aim is to continuously upgrade yourself and get bigger and better results from life

Once upon a time, there was a carpenter who had spent his life building houses from wood. He was past the age of retirement and was planning to quit his job and spend time with his family in peace. So, one day he asked his contractor if he could be relieved from his duties. The contractor insisted that he make one last house before he left. The carpenter said that would be fine. He would get some extra cash in his bank and the contractor would not push him to work too hard, this being his last assignment. Since, this was his last assignment, he was in a hurry to finish it, and so he ended up doing a real shoddy job, the nails were loose and the wood was not polished properly. Somehow the carpenter finished the work in a few days and told the contractor about it. The contractor then called the carpenter and said, "Here are the keys to your new home. This is a gift I wanted to give to you". The carpenter was horror struck!

That's how most people live their lives, unthinking and unaware of the consequences of their actions. People find it difficult to improve because they believe, quite falsely, that to do quality stuff you need to make massive changes in your life. On the contrary, it's not massive changes in your life, but small changes with massive courage that we need regularly. Focus on incremental improvement. Reading one article a day on a subject of your choice can make you a well-informed authority on the subject; in six months' time; giving a rose to your spouse, girlfriend or boyfriend can rekindle passion in your relationship; wishing a customer with a smiling face can result in a lasting relationship. Setting aside 15 minutes every day to thank God for what He has given can change your perspective.

Small increments add up to huge results. Think about how you can add value to your work or eliminate mistakes from it. You may also be able to do away with an unwanted task. Small yet consistent actions can help you take one giant step. Long-term effort and success require persistence, so think long-term. I have seen so many people exhausting themselves early because they are drained out during the initial phases of their journey. They believe improvement is a one-time event. But it is an ongoing process, wherein you need to put in effort, persist and experience the pain mentally before you can view yourself with changed eyes. Take up a common improvement program – a weight loss program. When an overweight person decides to improve his appearance, wants to tighten his muscles, chisel his physique and wear good clothes, he begins spending time in the gym. This is a lifestyle change because it includes dietary changes and changes in perception. This effort puts him through pain because he leaves his past behind and tries to become someone new.

His strength lies in his decisiveness to consistently work towards a goal. And as he persists, his thoughts and beliefs change. The person experiences joy after seeing himself in a new light. Ultimately, all *kaizen* is meant to make you feel the joy of change.

Create Value

Price is what you pay. Value is what you get.

–Warren Buffett

Would you marry someone you don't love? Most people will answer this question with an emphatic

'NO'. Nobody wants to marry someone they don't love because love for your partner is the foundation of a successful long-term loving relationship. If you don't want to marry someone you don't love, why engage in a career you don't love? After all, you will be spending around 60% to 70% of your life working; this is more than the time you will be spending with your spouse. Just as in your relationships, in your career too, long-term success is determined by the foundation you set.

Find your passion. This doesn't mean finding the thing you enjoy doing most. That's only the first criterion. The second criterion of living your passion is creating value for others by doing what you enjoy doing. Most people associate living their passion with ignoring materialistic necessities. Or sitting in a garage doing what others would call weird. Doing what you enjoy will only give you partial happiness. Your work needs to be of value to people, it is then that monetary rewards will begin to come in.

Find what you love to do and you won't have to work a single day

Though there are many ways of finding your passion, a few are practicable. One of these is to ask yourself specific questions:

- If you are given 100,000 dollars, what would you like to do with it?

- What would you do if you didn't have any problems in life?
- How would you spend your time if you were totally free of all your responsibilities?

Now if I were to answer these questions, I would have said, "I will buy a villa with a huge swimming pool, a five-star gymnasium with a small Jacuzzi, a Mercedes, and play volleyball and basketball every day, lazing around and sipping fresh lime soda in the summer heat with my beautiful spouse. And finally, I would put the rest of my money in my bank account and live off the interest". Simple!

Now that is unrealistic because I know I don't have that kind of money. So let me tell you the secret to living your passion. It is *to find a way to serve as many people as you can by doing what you love.* You can serve a certain number of people only when you can identify people who might need the sort of help you are able to provide. No matter what you love to do, find a way to fulfill the needs of people.

Serving means to be at service. To serve people and have financial security, you need to hone the skill of identifying a need and fulfilling it better than anyone else does.

Bill Gates was ridiculed when he said he dreamt of putting a computer on every desk. He anticipated a future need. He could do that because he was a visionary. Vision is how far ahead in time one can see. Today, Microsoft is a household name known by almost everyone.

It was an act of creating and fulfilling a need. Mark Zuckerberg, an Internet entrepreneur who fulfilled the needs of youngsters to be socially connected, founded Facebook, which is one of the world's biggest social networking websites. Google, an organization founded by Sergey Brin and Larry Page, dedicated itself to providing information to surfers across the world and today everything you can imagine is available on Google. Ultimately, it is all about creating value for others by serving them better than anyone else.

How incredible would you feel when you will be paid to live your passion! I have seen several examples, ranging from artists to musicians to photographers and dancers, who are paid well for doing what they love. For example, you like watching cricket but you cannot afford to watch cricket all your life without doing anything else. No one will pay you for that. But you may create value for people by providing relevant cricket data and statistics on a blog or you can even be a cricket commentator. Harsha Bhogle is someone who took his interest in cricket seriously and worked hard to hone his skills. And now that he is a success, companies pay him for doing what he enjoys. Undoubtedly, today he is one of the most successful and charismatic cricket commentators we love.

You need to market your skills and interests to create value for someone. Your passion is futile if left to languish at home. It's like keeping a Rolls Royce and not driving it. It belongs to the road, where it can flash in all its exuberance.

How does this help me?

1. You set the standards of your success.

   'Passion is not what you find,
   but what you create'

2. All limitations are those of an exhausted mind.

   'Limits are meant to be
   broken or transcended'

3. Unless you dream, you will never have what you want.

   'Dreams work only
   when you begin to work'

4. Compose your own life. Chart out your own destinations.

   'You don't need massive changes,
   you need massive courage'

5. Create value for others by doing what you love.

   'Let people pay you for
   living your passion'

CHAPTER 2
Purpose

The purpose of life is to have a life of purpose. Purpose creates energy and momentum. It gives life to the dead, courage to the dull and light to the dark. It transforms an individual completely because it provides meaning to life. There are two very important days in someone's life–the day he is born and the day he realizes why he was born.

Once a spiritual guru asked a monk in a monastery, "Dear son, how much have you lived?" and the monk replied "I have lived 32 years". The guru said, "How do you know you have lived 32 years?" The monk thought and replied, "That's my age". The guru again asked, "How much have you lived?" Now the monk was confused and replied, "I have lived for 32 years according to my date of birth". The guru replied, "Time is not the best measurement of life. I mean the moments you have lived with a purpose".

There are two ways people live their lives, one set of people live and the other set of people exist. What's the difference? Living means being aware of oneself and being able to answer the why of life. Only existing is being in a state of hypnosis. Life becomes a passage of time, without knowing how fast time runs. One day the hypnotic trance is broken, either their time has come to an end or a crisis has thrown them out of the hypnotic trance; and then they begin to find or create purpose in their lives.

Action should be purpose-driven. Actions produce results and results in turn create satisfaction. People who start their day without deciding the purpose of the day produce limited results. They mistake action for achievement. The greatest delusion of a man is to confuse being busy with being productive. The first step towards making your life joyous and content will be to guide yourself where you want to see yourself.

You may not know the purpose of your life but knowing that you are keen to find it is, in itself, a big achievement. Let me tell you that you are one among a handful of people across the world who not only know they have to find their purpose but have also picked up a book to make a change in their lives.

Life is a dance that is to be enjoyed by everyone. If you wish to master the art of dancing, you need to catch the rhythm of the music and the tunes which are being played. If music can be called a compilation of tunes, success is music and your life's purpose is the tune. If you can catch the tune, you can enjoy the music and the dance.

Make a Mark

Most men lead lives of quiet desperation and go to the grave with the song still in them.

–Henry David Thoreau

We are often driven by our past experiences. I would like to challenge you to live in the future today. I want you to imagine your funeral, with your soul observing the scene from the skies. You are lying on the funeral pyre surrounded by people who loved you, worked with you, and were close to you. Your soul can see people crying because they lost someone they loved. And when your obituary is written, everyone will know how you lived. It will mention the values which you stood for, the lives you touched, the difference you made to this world, and how well you lived your life.

Make a mark before you say good-bye

Your soul gets a chance to speak with God before it is finally liberated. He says, "For all the good work you have done I will give you the chance to write your own obituary and define how you would like to be remembered by people long after your demise. This is an opportunity very few souls get, and you are the lucky one. Redefine your life and give it a purpose."

Don't wait for that moment. Wake up and redesign your life now.

The best place to be when you have lost meaning in your life is a graveyard, where you will see unfulfilled dreams, wasted talent, missed opportunities, burnt-out passions and dejection lingering around.

In today's world,

- Workers resign long before handing their resignation letters in.
- Lovers become lonely long before their partners leave them.
- People die in their 20s and are buried in their 60s or 70s.
- Sportsmen become engineers and engineers become doctors.

There is chaos everywhere; people are stuck in dangerous patterns. But nature abhors imbalance. She balances fire with water, rain with sunlight, humans with animals and birds, air with vacuum, day with night, summers with winters, happiness with sadness et al.

Nature has created the most powerful balance that can guide us in times of despair – it's the balance of life and death. You can use these balanced powers to your advantage

Let us speak of a man who stood for this balance. He was an innovator, an entrepreneur, a cancer survivor, a husband, a colleague, a guru. He is Steve Jobs, co-founder of Apple. What you don't know about him is the question he asked himself daily. It's called the Steve Jobs Question. During his Commencement address at Stanford, he shared a philosophy which directs his actions and thoughts on a daily basis with the students there. Every morning he asked himself this question–

'If today were the last day of my life, would I want to do what I am about to do today?' This question can move anyone from his routine functions to rethink and get back on the track to a significant life by connecting you with your inner being and preventing your ego from taking decisions on your behalf. You are driven by your conscience the moment you realize this might be the last day of your life and you are not afraid of defeat and failure because they look very small in the face of death.

One day this question will be the truth of our lives. And if we are guided by our own inner compass, our lives will be genuine.

One question humans have never been able to answer is 'Is there a way to live forever?' Thousands of scientists, researchers and spiritual gurus have spent their lives searching for the answer. People have travelled across countries and continents to unravel the secret to immortality. Sometimes, the most complex questions have the simplest of answers. The secret of living forever is to make a visible, audible and tangible mark with the purpose of your life. But purpose is something that has to be created, it can't be found.

What you want is more important than what you don't want

What Do You Really Want?

All achievements, all earned riches, have their beginning in an idea.

–Napoleon Hill

Ask someone what they want and they give you a list of things they don't want. We do not want debts, divorces, credit bills, hatred and insecurity; these are the common answers. These people have decided to focus on what they don't want but does our mind work like that?

There is a famous saying, "You attract the things that you focus on". When someone says I don't want delayed payments, you know what he will get – delayed payments. This is called the law of attraction and it works twenty four hours a day. The law is a long-drawn concept and it is also features in the book *The Secret* by Rhonda Byne and I recommend it if you want to study the concept in detail, but for now, let's get back to those people who always focus on what they don't want and then they actually get what they don't want. They need to consistently focus on things they want for there to be an instant paradigm shift.

Successful people focus on what they want, and the rest focus on what they don't want. Ask yourself what kind of things you would like to have around your workplace, in your school, at home, in your business and if possible, write them down. Maybe you want a better relationship or more money. My first suggestion is you begin focusing on what you want and not what you don't want because the law of attraction is working every moment. That brings us to the next question–

What do you *really* want?

A kind of caterpillar called 'processionary caterpillars' were experimented on. Their names came from a character trait they possessed – that of following their leader wherever the leader moved. In the experiment they were placed in a circle, where the leader was placed in such a position that he was after the last caterpillar in the arrangement. Then they started to move one after the other in the circle and their favorite food was placed in the middle of the circle. Though the food was placed within their reach, they were moving one after the other without knowing what they want. They followed each other day after day thinking that they were on the right path. One day, they gave up, exhausted. The food had been a few inches away.

Are we very different from the caterpillars? Do we understand that we keep on moving in the same direction, conforming to our environment, just like the processionary caterpillars and fail to recognize that we want something else? The food which we fail to recognize is food for our soul and heart.

In this utter confusion and imbalance, people need to take a break for some soul searching and asking themselves what they really want. Recognise the patterns around you in which people are stuck: when engineering is a popular course, everyone studies engineering and sticks to this pattern only to follow each other into a trap.

The painter becomes an engineer, the engineer becomes a doctor, the doctor becomes a salesman and no one is happy because they follow others instead of fueling their own dreams and desires. This is also known as the herd mentality.

There is no better joy than in finding what you want and working to achieve it; it vitalizes you and you feel alive again. Remember that life is short and someone somewhere is breathing his last. You are the lucky one with the opportunity to decide what you want in your life.

Don't follow trends, be the trend

What Can You Learn from Children?

The great man is he who does not lose his child's heart.

–Mencius, Book IV

Do you remember the time you were a child, bursting with energy and enthusiasm, curious about the zillion things surrounding you? You dreamed of amazing things, shamed scientists with your imagination and twisted and turned your body the way you wanted. It was just phenomenal.

Our talents accompany us from our birth but we fail to work on them. Whatever you don't use is either wasted or worn out and we are left with people who can dream but lack the conviction to work for their dreams. On the other hand, there are some people who have also completely lost the ability to dream. They are so caught up in the rhythm of their past conditioning that they have lost touch with themselves. They don't know what they want because they haven't looked within.

Have you ever hopped onto a bandwagon? Don't say no, because you may have not been on the bandwagon literally, but our minds travel places. In older times bandwagons were used to carry band people from cities to circuses. That would attract people watching them to join the bandwagon and lure them to visit the circus. Similarly, if a few people choose to go a particular way, others begin to follow them. Children are trendsetters, they do new things; they make toys out of soap and use a cape to play a superhero.

Be aware of your life choices, you do not have to do what others ask you to do. Leave the bandwagon of societal conformance. A child is different from an adult because he does not want to mindlessly follow norms; as he grows up he wants to use his imagination but he is afraid. His beliefs have been changed drastically by his friends, his family, his colleagues and the expectations of his spouse.

See the difference below:

When you were a child–

- You searched for things you wanted and were curious about your environment.

- You did things you loved doing and you reacted spontaneously, without judging anyone.
- You asked for help when you needed it and dreamt of places you wanted to visit.

Today

- You seek things accepted by your social circle and avoid goals that may be too challenging.
- You dislike your job because it is meaningless and you react carefully, after analyzing all possible consequences.
- You never ask for help because it makes you feel weak and your only dream is that of survival.

It was the continuous conditioning that made the difference. In your childhood, you were conditioned by your friends when they said you could never be a superhero or when your neighbor asked you not to cross the fence or when your teacher forced you to paint though you always wanted to sculpt.

The story changed a little after you became an adult. Your colleagues said it was more important to hold onto your job than to fulfill your dreams but working too hard wasn't good either because then you would be called a workaholic. If you took up a hobby and tried to make it your career society would mock you to damnation.

And with all this conditioning the great transformation took place. A liberated, fearless, daring and innovative child became a feeble, incapacitated, fearful and unsatisfied adult. If you cut off your ideas, thoughts and dreams of realizing yourself, you are committing suicide. Life doesn't take years to change, it can change in moments. This is your moment, go ahead and take the plunge.

Let Your Sails Fly

> *When there is freedom from mechanical conditioning, there is simplicity. The classical man is just a bundle of routine, ideas and tradition. If you follow the classical pattern, you are understanding the routine, the tradition, the shadow, you are not understanding yourself.*
>
> –Bruce Lee

The ones who refuse to condition themselves according to the ways of the world are the most successful people on this planet. They refuse to accept self-defeating norms, the limiting beliefs and trivial goals; they challenge these norms, stand for their beliefs and never give up till they are the stars of their own show. I call them champions. Champions are individuals

> *Be a champion, live a champion's life, die a champion*

with positive self-conditioning who consistently develop new ways of thinking that empower them to make wise choices in difficult times; thereby getting the best out of situations life has to offer. They are neither withered away by their competitor's potential nor by the expectations of others because they are their only competitors. They find their answers in books, movies, magazines and other sources. They ask for help, they learn from others. They read empowering and positive books. They ask how it can be done instead of justifying why it cannot be done and their performance, too, is result-oriented. Nothing is impossible for them; they rule their destiny.

The other set of people condition themselves negatively: I call them prisoners, people who confine themselves within their homes by creating artificial iron bars of negative thoughts around themselves. They resemble weeds, which choke blossoming plants and eventually cause harm to the ground on which they grow. Negative thoughts have the potential to destroy the garden of your mind by ruining your carefully-grown positivity and confidence. The prisoner looks at the world through dark-tinted glasses, finding fault with everything and associating positive events with negative vibes. Individuals need acceptance and they will stop taking risks if that is what it takes to be part of their social circle.

Their environment shapes their behavior, habits and thoughts negatively till they find comfort in their destructive routine and reject all chances of growth that come their way. For example, if they were sexually abused as children, they will look out for situations where others have undergone the same experience and will focus only those situations in which the people have suffered and destroyed their lives, instead of focusing on those references where they have come out very well and have transformed their lives for the greater good. Such people cut the branch on which they sit instead of watering and fertilizing their own tree of life.

Decide once and for all that you will take complete control of your life and you will positively condition your mind with all the enriching influences around you and within you. If you don't plan your life, others will plan it for you and it will not be a good one. Read good books, watch well-made films and expose your mind to the wealth of positivity all around you. How you use your mind affects your life in certain ways but what is most important is that you have to decide where to go on your own.

Lead Before You Manage

Management is doing things right; leadership is doing the right things.

–Peter Drucker

Most people we know are just managers, trying to manage their lives. Very few are leaders of their own life and it is because they have left the task of leadership to someone else, probably their boss, their deity, the society, the parents, the friends and to many others.

Take the example of someone who wishes to climb Mount Everest. He has travelled from his home to Nepal to begin his sojourn and he is alone on this journey, carrying with himself his sophisticated equipment, high precision tools, special winter clothing, a tent and sufficient supply of food. The way he manages his resources will affect the result he achieves but a mountaineer cannot carry everything; he has to store supplies so he can make it to his destination and come back safely. The skill it takes to carry the minimum resources and use it optimally is called resource management.

But what if you don't have a compass which shows you the direction you have to move towards, what will you do with your resources?

Leadership first, management second

You will be going from mountain to mountain without knowing your destination, your resources will deplete and one day you will be in serious trouble. For mountaineers, the most important thing while climbing a mountain is to have a compass so that they can move in the right direction and if they are off course they can again come back to the base camp and equip themselves better for the journey again.

In life, every person has a mountain to conquer, and the great God has given each one of us specific tools and equipments in the form of our talents and skills to help us reach our destination. But he has not given us the most important equipment, the compass, which shows us where we have to go. The compass shows where we have to go. You were born to be a painter and you are working with medicine or you should be a sportsman and you are trying to make it in accountancy. Why are you climbing the wrong mountain?

People live as if they are on a survival program. They survive bills, loans, payments, credit and luxury, living through a test everyday without knowing when supplies might be cut off. But they forget they're equipped for the struggle but survival does not equal achievement.

Some are happy just counting days and months while asking themselves how they work at something they don't really like.

Leading in life means taking the correct direction and picking up the compass to decide which route to take. No amount of resources can help you reach your destination unless you know where to go. Once you know your destination, you can manage your resources. Ask yourself:

- What do I want from my life emotionally, cerebrally, socially, physically and financially?
- What am I living for? What will be my contribution to the world?

Be clear about your direction and then concentrate on managing your resources. It is necessary to lead and manage effectively but we tend to confuse activity with accomplishment. You may be working long hours and doing your work well but what if you're doing the wrong job? It may mean you're doing something unfulfilling and ultimately unproductive. The process that you follow to achieve results should be efficient and the goal you choose to pursue determines your effectiveness.

What is the formula of success? The first step is to decide where you want to reach and what fulfils you. The second step is to find the right means, resources, tools and strategies to maximize results.

How does this help me?

1. Ask yourself the Steve Jobs question everyday.

   'If today were the last day of my life,
   would I want to do what
   I am about to do today?'

2. Don't confuse activity with accomplishment.

   'First, know what you want!'

3. Don't join others on their journey.

   'Create your own way'

4. Become a champion, write your own destiny.

   'Direct your life towards
   a meaningful destination'

5. Become a leader by being effective.

   'Stop surviving and start living'

CHAPTER 3
Productivity

Success is the ability to produce. It's the ability to produce products, services, goods, satisfaction, energy and experience. Without production, you cannot contribute. Be like the farmer who knows that to produce means to add value to the world. A farmer does his bit by planting the seeds of his actions at the right place at the right time. If the place is not right, he will not be able to reap the harvest. If the time is not right, he won't get the seeds to grow. But you can be different from the farmer. One does not need to wait for the right time to plant the seeds of action; every moment is the right moment. You cannot change the past; today is the only day which is given to you to produce something of value to the world.

But you cannot get a good harvest just by planting the seeds. You need to have the skill of anticipation, which means being aware of and prepared for possible challenges. It's like moving from reaction to response. By nurturing your garden the right way, you don't need to wait till the weeds appear. If you are new to farming, don't worry! Go and find someone who has learned to reap the best harvest in town. If he can do it, you can do it.

You need to be consistent in your efforts. You can't leave the process in between! If you leave your land without watering it at the right times, you will not reap anything. The seeds might die.

Sometimes you will have to travel the extra mile too! The extra mile may just take you to the next town for strategy, information, equipment and skills. You can't afford to stay in your own town without making an effort to know what is the best and the fastest way to produce.

Competition is so stiff. Once the harvest has been reaped, you need to make sure that it reaches the marketplace before your competitors. Don't wait for life to happen to you; make the most of what you have instead. Lou Holtz said, "Life is ten percent what happens to you and ninety percent how you respond to it."

Respond to life before it's too late, learn the skills needed to reap a good harvest, know the best tools needed to produce, don't wait for life to happen.

Learn to Anticipate

As Daddy said, life is 95 percent anticipation.

–Gloria Swanson, actress

A schoolboy once asked his cricket coach, "How can I become a great fielder?" The coach pointed towards the batsman and said, "Anticipate where the batsman is going to hit the ball and where the ball will go. If you can anticipate what's going to come in future, you can prepare yourself for it. If you are ready, you will be active and if you are active, you will grab the ball." Anticipation is the key in life. Anticipate where your relationships are headed, anticipate how your business is going to progress and anticipate the direction of your career. It is a natural process. We anticipate all the time, but we do not do it consciously.

We anticipate our manager's mood before meeting him in the morning. Our parents anticipate the financial needs of the family before doing their financial planning. Students anticipate what questions their teacher might ask them, a husband anticipates how his wife is going to react when he returns late while a salesman anticipates the objections that a client may put up. Boxers anticipate the next hit during a tournament. But all such anticipation is unconscious. We need to do this consciously and at the right places.

The greatest skill you can possess is the skill to anticipate challenges and changes. Michael Dell, founder of Dell Inc., was using his power of assumption when he started directly shipping computers to the consumers, thus doing away with middle men. So, the computers were cheap and they suited the needs of certain consumers. He anticipated the business needs of his domain better than others in his industry. Today, he is a very influential man who is a celebrated CEO, an author, and has been featured on the Forbes Billionaire list too. Ask yourself, "What would happen if I keep on doing the same things again and again? Will my life today be any different from yesterday?" People who are doing well in any area of their lives, have learned to correctly predict their future and change their courses accordingly.

Anticipate future challenges and solve them now

There are people who anticipate an opportunity and act instantly to reap its results. A worker in a manufacturing unit knew that an expansion was going to take place and the company would need a supervisor. So, he invested in being trained as a supervisor. When the opportunity came, he was the first person to be promoted by the company and it happened because he anticipated the opportunity and instinctively acted on it.

My friend had made huge profits investing in stocks. One day, I asked him the secret of his consistent success to which he replied, "Anticipate the future of a company and invest today. People who cannot anticipate correctly should never invest in stocks." Stockbrokers charge people heavily for telling them where to invest and they are able to do it because they possess this particular skill – that of correctly anticipating market trends.

Anticipate what might happen in a year, both in your professional and your personal life, in three and five years. If you have a business, how will it change? What skill changes would arrive in your domain? What new technology will make a breakthrough? Where will new markets develop? When will the economy boom for your business to prosper? By asking these questions, you get an idea of the future. It may not be one hundred percent accurate, but it readies you for impending change. Why did so many people lose their jobs in the 2010-12 recession? Because they couldn't anticipate where the markets were headed; when the banks were wiped out, most of them were bankrupt.

When you know what's lying ahead, you either change your course or correct yourself so that you arrive at the right destination in style. Become like Larry Page and Sergey Brin, the founders of Google, who anticipated the need for information availability through the Internet and invented the world's best search engine.

If you can anticipate ten or twenty years ahead, it's a great skill but if you're not a fortune teller, you don't need to look that far. Take baby steps and try seeing six months ahead. You don't need to see the entire staircase to reach your destination; you can have a successful journey if you look only five or six steps ahead.

Let us suppose that I ask you to walk from one corner of the room to the other corner; you will be easily able to do so. You might even take bold steps, but what if I blindfold you? Won't you then take baby steps? Many people fail to see the next step too; they don't know what's lying ahead. Is there any obstruction? Is there a bend in the road? Does the path change? They take random steps forward. Become proactive, *see it before it comes.* To make a successful building, you need to have the blueprint in mind and act according to the blueprint. Walt Disney died in 1966, five years before Disneyland was open to the public. A reporter, at the launch of Disneyland, said to Roy Disney, "It's too bad Walt did not live to see this." Roy replied, "Walt saw it first. That's why you are seeing it now". See the future in your mind and try to foresee how your life may challenge you.

Plan Your Day

You were born to win, but to be a winner, you must plan to win, prepare to win, and expect to win.

–Zig Ziglar

Failing to plan is planning to fail. There must have been days in your life when you might have said to yourself, "A whole day has passed by but I haven't done anything!", or, "I have been working since morning and it's evening now! When will I start doing some real work!" These words are proof of the fact that we do not plan our days; a planned day implies finishing all tasks and asking ourselves what we should do next!

Planning and prioritizing your day is no rocket science. Many authors have shared their philosophy on this subject by dividing time into various complex quadrants and then asking the reader to prioritize and plan his/her work accordingly. In this fast-paced world, where every moment counts, making such a detailed plan may be difficult. It would also be time-consuming to keep track of it throughout the day so it would be a good idea to suggest something that works easily.

In our mundane lives, we fail to understand the importance of prioritizing our work. We do the easier things first and leave the more important and complicated things for the rest of the day. We fail to complete our work within the time we have and we complain about not having enough time. Successful people follow a simple principle–

> *Things which matter most must never be at the mercy of things which matter least.*
>
> –Johann Wolfgang von Goethe

They firmly believe in tackling the most critical tasks first thing in the morning, so that when these are over, they can take up other tasks without any mental pressure. The trick is to keep our mind stress-free. When you do the unimportant tasks first, the fact that you still have major tasks to complete weigh us down. This mental pressure lowers your productivity. You fail both to focus on your task and to commit yourself to it. Use the several planning apps available online – the planners available in bookstores or you can buy a Daily Planner where you can make a list of all the things you have to do the next day. Jim Rohn, author of *The Keys to Success*, points out, "Don't start your day until it is finished on paper."

Do the things which matter most

You should only let your memory serve you when you need it; you need not rely on it for everything.

Keep the high-priority tasks on top of your Daily Planner and then write about the things which are not that important. Every morning, glance through your daily planner and plan your day. You will be amazed at the quality of commitment you would be able to give to every task if you follow such a process. As you go on completing the tasks, keep on ticking off the task in your planner. By the end of the day, gauge your performance and see where you could have saved more time and done some more valuable work. The key is to try to improve your planning capabilities each day.

Always remember you have the power to DASE-

Delegate

Automate

Segregate

Eliminate

Delegate

Find the right person to do things for you, so that you have that buffer time to perform well, develop a skill or educate yourself about new things as well as earn more. You don't have to do all the things in the world; you only need to focus on fulfilling activities.

Automate

Use technology wherever possible to reduce manual intervention. People who are not comfortable with technology will find it difficult to cope with the present technologically-oriented lifestyle. Use tablets, documentation softwares and applications in your mobile to keep track of various activities on the go.

Segregate

Set yourself small goals, accomplish one thing at a time, see things in their entirety and thereby, reduce the pressure. Break down big tasks into bite-sized activities and start taking action on one action at a time.

Eliminate

Eliminate the tasks which do not add value to your performance or to the people around you and delete useless tasks, or tasks you do not want to do. Useless tasks engage us daily and due to our busy schedule, we don't get the time to think whether the activity is useful or not. In the process, we forget that we are wasting our talents by doing profitless work.

Planning serves two purposes – firstly, you allocate time for all activities and secondly, you keep yourself in control. The most crucial aspect of our lives is to have clarity of thought. To be uncertain and unsure of what we want to achieve in life could be one of the biggest hindrances to attaining success. Planning your life means you drive your life, you are the master of the circus that your life is and you are the king of your kingdom. Do you remember the last time when you were certain? Maybe, you were sure of reaching your office or your college in time today. Weren't you relaxed because you were in control of your circumstances? If you are not used to this feeling, you might feel slightly victorious and if you are consistent, a series of small victories might turn into a massive gain someday.

Be in control of your destiny even if your plans don't work out. Planning is not aimed to accomplish your goals or help you succeed, though it does contribute in a big way; the real reason of planning is developing self-management skills but, like any other muscle, it takes time to develop. Further, it requires consistent effort. I made so many plans for my life but only a few of them materialized. This happens because we are guided by an invisible force which controls the outcomes of our lives. When you expect something to happen, something else pops up instead. *Consistent planning can work wonders.* Change your approach and your plan if you don't get the desired results. Be flexible while charting your map to success.

The First Step Is to Take the First Step

The elevator to success is out of order. You'll have to use the stairs... one step at a time.

–Joe Girard

The power to take the first step is the power which will give you the momentum required to begin the journey towards your goals. It is just as if there are ten steps to your destination, and with the very first step, you begin to reduce the distance between your today and your tomorrow. Everything around us, from the chair you're sitting on to the laptop you use daily, has been made possible because someone took the first step someday.

A good start is half the job done

Imagine being on a cross country travel in your car. How do you begin? You get into your car, start the engine, put the vehicle in the first gear and accelerate. Gradually, as time progresses and you find a way, you decide to shift to higher gears. And, as you move forward, you begin to observe other aspects of the journey, such as road conditions, traffic and the weather. Today is the time to put your vehicle in the first gear, and begin your life. Once you have gained momentum, you can measure your growth by reviewing your dashboard, looking carefully at the traffic ahead, sorting out your priorities, and being aware of the excess work to be done. Don't stop your car in the middle of the road, try to maneuver it, or get on the highway whenever you are off track. Once the going gets easy and you see small successes coming your way, it is time for you to shift gears and develop a new set of goals.

Fred Smith, the founder of the world's leading delivery company, took his first step when he wrote about his idea (of overnight delivery) in his project and got a C minus for it from the professor. But he didn't measure his entrepreneurial journey with the first grade he received; according to him, the first step took him a little closer to his dream. He persisted, took more such steps, and having gained momentum, he took stronger and faster steps. In this way, he started off with his own business and he finally established one of the world's biggest companies. The greatest problem faced by men and women, today, is that they measure themselves by their first step; they generalize specifics.

Think if any of these situations is applicable to you:

- You confronted your lover after he/she had rejected you. You probably never found the courage to confront them.
- You tried to give a presentation after you had failed to make a good impression the first time around. You probably believed you were not good enough.
- You opened your heart out to someone, and when he/she couldn't live up to your standards, you snapped all ties with him/her.

- You told someone how much you loved them and when they didn't reciprocate, you stopped communicating with them.
- You tried to pursue your interest and you failed. You must have told yourself, "I am not worth it".

Don't generalize life – let specifics remain specifics and keep on moving in the direction that you have sought for yourself without judging yourself for it. It is only when we judge ourselves too early that we lose our true selves.

We may believe that nothing is happening after our first step fails, but every step has its own significance. It is the question of the growth of the bamboo tree. Does it take five years to grow or five weeks? Initially you may not see any improvement when you water the bamboo plant, but this is the time when its roots are growing within the ground. Success doesn't come in a moment; it comes after many moments of hard work.

Don't wait. People wait for situations to be perfect, to acquire all thc resources, to learn the right set of skills and while waiting, we believe we are doing the right thing. This is a delusion because we spend a lot of time thinking about what we want to do. You can never reach your goal only by thinking. It is the first step that gives you momentum.

Cricket players strategize before they go on the field, and when they are on the field, they perform as per the game plan. If and when things do not work according to strategies, they take their own decisions while playing on the basis of other variables: if they see batsmen attacking, they devise a strategy to limit the runs being scored by making appropriate fielding and bowling changes. They strategize before the game, and then restrategize during the game; the scoreboard gives them continuous feedback. Planning is not a one-time activity, it's a continuous process.

The first step one should take is to get oneself into the game and then one must learn to be spontaneous and flexible enough to change his plans according to the circumstances. As the cricket players cannot prepare for everything before getting on to the field, nobody can have entirely foolproof ideas and plans. Don't just depend on what you see, make use of your foresight after you have taken your first step. The first step is the precursor to winning the game.

The Extra Mile Effect

There are no traffic jams on the extra mile.

–Zig Ziglar

Water transforms into steam at 100 degrees, but at 99 degrees, the water is still boiling. A one-degree increase in temperature is enough to transform water into steam and this steam is then used to run engines and turbines, to produce electricity, to dry clean wet things and to heat buildings. There are many uses of steam but it is the one-degree temperature increase that transforms water into steam. Let me challenge you to replicate that one-degree change in your life. Exert yourself a little more while doing anything that you do; it is just one degree that differentiates water from steam.

The question you need to ask yourself everyday is "How am I different from everyone else?" If you find there is none, then you need to turn up the temperature a little more. Work hard at whatever you do and a little more; a little more effort is what it takes to become different. Many people are very close to their destination when they give up on life. They believe that hard work won't pay, they won't reach their dream, but they only need to work a little more.

Once, a farmer was told that there was plenty of gold underneath his land, so he began to dig it up. He dug for months, but was unable to find any gold. He worked hard, but eventually grew tired. When he was certain that there was no gold, he sold the land to his friend. His friend thought of digging the land a little more. He dug the land for a couple of hours and he saw something shining. It was gold. The friend was now rich. The previous owner had failed to dig the ground a little more and that made all the difference. When you are tired and want to give up, think about 'the little more' you can do to make a difference.

The story doesn't end here. The previous owner, who had worked hard yet failed to reap the harvest, regretted it. Regret is painful. When you know you could have put in a little extra effort and achieved what you wanted but you didn't because you gave up, the regret you experience will be more painful than walking the extra mile.

Extra degree of heat separates the water from the steam

When life ends, people don't feel sad about the things that they did. They regret the things they didn't do. As Whittier said, "Of all sad words of tongue or pen, the saddest are these, "It might have been".

If only I would have asked this girl out, I would have had a completely different relationship. If only I had worked a little more in office, I would have been promoted. If only I would have asserted myself, the contract would have been successful. If only I would have appreciated my employees, they would not have left me. If only I had a plan, I would not have been in trouble. Eliminate this phrase from your life by going the extra mile and making that one-degree change in your life. You will never regret having walked the extra mile.

For those who have not started on their paths to success, and curious about how to travel the extra mile, the answer would be to walk the required distance before setting off on the extra mile. You will have to make an effort to boil the water to 99 degrees before it reaches a stage where it is ready for transformation. Make an effort to reach 99 degrees in your career, relationships and social life and have a clear understanding of how it looks. For some, it might look like generating the highest sales in a department or successfully reducing a large number of errors in a short period of time or being promoted or making a ten-crore profit in a month.

It may also be attaining the desired shape of your body or being energetic throughout the day or loving your partner with all you have. You must decide your goal and work day by day towards achieving it. Once you think you have reached 99 degrees, ask yourself, "What can I do now to take my life to the next level?" Go beyond the expected. The most happy and loyal customers are the ones who have been served beyond their expectations and lasting relationships are possible only when partners go beyond the expected routine. You are perfectly healthy only when you look beyond your body and focus on your spiritual health.

Once you have gone the extra mile, don't stop, because a new journey begins there. People succeed because they have the ability to give their best every time they perform. The key is consistency; be consistent even after you have gone the extra mile. Anyone can perform once, but success comes only to those who can replicate their success again and again. You might have broken a world record while you were practicing, but it's of no use if you are not able to break the record at the real event. Consistency comes from practice so create the right time instead of waiting for it. Always remind yourself that when you are not practicing, someone somewhere is practicing and when you meet him, be ready for a hard challenge. Live to be and have the best in life. The greatest investment you can make in your life is to invest in your skills and talents by continuous practice. Pursue the extra mile.

Don't settle for mediocrity. Mediocrity breeds mediocrity. Performance has two levels – one that is expected and one beyond the expected level. Work hard to reach your expectations and move beyond those expectations to transform yourself. Expect the best from yourself and you will receive the best.

Get a Coach

All coaching is, is taking a player where he can't take himself.

–Bill McCartney, former American football player and coach

Who is a *guru*? *Guru*, a Sanskrit word, comes from two words, *gu* and *ru*. *Gu* implies the darkness of ignorance, while *ru* means the one who removes the darkness. A *guru* is the one who removes the darkness created by ignorance. For centuries, the relationship between a *guru* and his *shishya* has eliminated the darkness spread by ignorance and guided students to gain knowledge. In the past, education was privileged and students would go to a master and ask to be educated by him. If the master believed that the student deserved it, the master would teach the student. Times have changed and the web gives us free information. In the twenty-first century, a person doesn't have to wait for the *guru* to teach him something, he will Google it instead.

The guru eliminates ignorance through light

There is information overload today; there are so many sources of knowledge that it becomes hard to select which to notice and which to ignore. And the student, again, has to go to the master, not asking for information but for asking which information is useful and which is not.

The *guru* is no longer a person sitting under a tree discoursing on life. He is the one who has been there, done that and is experienced not because he knows everything, but because he knows which knowledge is right for you. Today's *guru* not only knows what should be done, but also knows what should not be done; he knows the rules and the strategies needed to achieve the success you are after. You don't need to go through the trial and error phase, though that is also a good method of learning. You can simply know the strategy and use it in your life to get the same quality of results your coach had achieved. We don't have all the time in the world to make useful mistakes and learn from them. Not only do you need to learn from coaches who have become successful, but also learn from coaches who have failed. One needs to know how to succeed and how to avoid failures. This is having all-round knowledge.

Having a coach doesn't mean you have to meet him or her. Coaches are available in libraries; they are available via emails, in articles, in newspapers and on the television. Find a coach who is a master in the area in which you wish to succeed. I have several coaches I have never met. I see my coaches in leaders like Robert Kiyosaki, Bill Gates, Jack Canfield, Robin Sharma and many more. I haven't had a chance to meet them, but

I have read their books, seen their videos, and listened to their audio programs. I learn from the way they deliver their messages, the way they write books and the way they market themselves. I chose them as my coaches because they are the best in their industry and they have achieved the success I want to achieve in this industry.

A few people have role models. And that's a good strategy because you enable yourself to go one step ahead of adopting strategies and look at the beliefs, values and philosophies of these people. Strategies of success stem from deep-rooted beliefs and values of people. If you have a role model, don't only use his strategy for your success; find out the underlying beliefs that made him or her develop the strategy. There is a Chinese proverb, *Give a man a fish and you feed him for a day. Teach a man how to fish and you feed him for a lifetime.* Don't just imitate short-term strategies of your role models, but know the beliefs behind their strategies. If you want to have a role model, here is what you should look for:

- Strategies: You must find out what strategies the role model uses to achieve his outcome. The context may be different. You can always use the framework of his strategy, tweaking bits of it to use it in your life. Strategies are the quickest way to get results; if one person has done it, you can do it too.

- Beliefs: What beliefs does the person have? What does he think before, during and after his performance? What does the role model say to himself? How does he condition his mind? Feelings precede actions; the right feeling can lead to the right actions.
- Values: Know the values of your role model. Values are the principles important to him or her. Values influence behavior and thoughts. You will get to know how your role model prioritizes his tasks and what aspects of life he focuses on. Gandhi valued peace and all his actions were driven by peace. Steve Jobs valued innovation and Albert Einstein valued imagination. Both of them achieved mastery in their respective fields. Know these values and see how you can apply the values of your role model.

A coach may not necessarily have all the experience you need. There is no perfect human being in this world and no one person can have all the experiences of life. Learn from every kind of coach while you design your philosophy of life. Variety is the spice of life and you should have a variety of information from your teachers, mentors and coaches. Once you have received information from everyone, you decide what is best for you.

What's in this for me?

1. Anticipate future challenges and solve them now.

   'See it before it happens'

2. Failing to plan is planning to fail.

   'Don't spend major time on minor tasks'

3. Don't judge too early, the first step is not the final one.

   'Take massive steps towards your destination'

4. The extra mile differentiates you from the rest.

   'Eliminate the phrase 'if only' from your life'

5. Study life.

   'Learn from the ones who have succeeded and from the ones who have failed'

CHAPTER 4

Perception

Your mind is like a parachute which works only when it is open. Open your mind to the possibilities life has to offer. Look around yourself – whatever you see was a creation of a mind before it became a reality. Ask a painter about the first time he painted something beautiful and his answer would be 'In my mind'. Paint your future in your mind, before you paint it in reality. There are various shades of life and you need to know how to play around these shades to get the perfect picture of your life; visualize how you want life to unfold, how you want the colors of different aspects of your life to combine and give you a good picture.

You have the choice to see a half empty or a half full glass. You may say half full or half empty, if you see it half empty you can have a better perspective of seeing it half full. But can you see the glass better than half full too. One may also say that the glass is completely full, one half with water and the other half with air. The choice is always yours. It all depends on where your focus is.

Our fears are imaginary because they are a creation of our mind. We are so busy seeing the glass half empty that we don't realize that it is also half full. Fear can be an acronym for both 'Fall every time and run'or 'Face everything and rise'. If you run away from your fears, they will always run with you because they are in your mind. Condition your mind not to think positively but intelligently. See the reality as it is, instead of making it worse than it is. See the future with extreme optimism; let it open windows to new possibilities. Two salesmen of a shoe manufacturing company went to Zambia to examine the market potential of the place. They came back and stated their findings. The first salesman said, "There is no potential. Nobody wears shoes there". The other salesman said, "There is huge potential. Nobody wears shoes there". It all depends on how you see it – as an opportunity or a difficulty?

Sometimes we don't understand why things turn out the way they do. You don't need to understand how life works, you only need to see the things happening around you as feedback to your own actions and remember actions may include both cerebral and emotional actions. It has long been established that every action has an equal and opposite reaction. If you think positive, whatever you receive is positive. If you think negative, then you get results accordingly. As you sow, so shall you reap and whatever you give will eventually come back to you. But the good news is that everything starts from the mind. You can condition your mind to set positive causes in action through positive thinking.

Much of the negativity in your circumstances has been created by your mind. Change the way you think and you will see that the world will change for you.

Fear Will Lower Your Possibilities of Success

Nothing in life is to be feared. It is only to be understood.

–Marie Curie

As the brake is to a car, fear is to success. Imagine you are accelerating your wagon of success on the journey to your goal and suddenly you apply the brake, but the accelerator is still pushed to the hilt. What will happen? The wagon will heat up and it might even break down. Similarly, when you fear something, you tend to apply mental brakes to your mind, which will heat you up till you break down.

The greatest challenge people face is when they live a life of resistance. Resisting uncomfortable situations is the real cause of fear. What you will resist will always persist. I remember a time I was asked to give a presentation in my college, and I used to believe that being onstage would be a loss of the reputation I had among my friends. I had to face the situation because there was no other option. When facing your fears is a must, you need to confront them; only then will all your anxieties perish.

Run towards your fears

You are no longer uncertain about whether or not to face it. You have to face your fear, and this shift unleashes your greatest strength lying dormant inside. With this shift from a 'may have' to a 'must', I was able to fare decently at the event while also being appreciated by my friends. When I reached my hostel at the end of the day, I realized that fear was my own creation that had hindered me from moving ahead; it was then that I concluded that fear was a manifestation of our imagination and appears to be real because of their sheer negativity. Fear is an illusion in which people get trapped and fail to see reality. Fear comes in many shapes and sizes, but after giving it immense thought, I have found out that there are three basic reasons of fear which create barriers in the path of victory–

- Fear of rejection
- Fear of the unknown
- Fear of failure

Fear of rejection

Don't say 'yes' to rejection, say 'next' instead. More the number of rejections, greater are your chances of success. JK Rowling, the acclaimed author of the Harry Potter books, was rejected by many publishers before one of them agreed to publish the first Harry Potter book. The rest is history. Walt Disney had been rejected by a newspaper because he apparently lacked creative genius and Sylvester Stallone kept going till he was allowed to play the lead role in 'Rocky', which incidentally was his own script! When you are faced with rejection, don't accept it. Instead, wait for your next opportunity, knowing you are about to get the monumental success you were waiting for.

Fear of the unknown

Harland David Sanders had a belief that his pressurized cooking style of chicken would be highly popular among people and his recipe would be one of the best in the market. He was entering into an unknown terrain with his new cooking style and a completely different recipe. Not many people know that he failed to sell his recipe an approximate 1009 times before his recipe was accepted by a restaurant[1]. He found a completely new market with his recipe because he dared to venture with his recipe into the unknown market, which accepted him after his long drawn efforts. He then founded the popular food chain KFC, also known as Kentucky Fried Chicken which today is one of the leading fast food joints. Having a belief is the key to grazing on unknown pastures. Obviously, you are going to face lots of challenges but also know that you are going to receive the fruit of being the first innovator in the field. Sanders believed in his cooking style and his recipe, and with this belief he entered an unknown market. It is in the unknown that your true potential lies. Believe in your thoughts and ideas.

Fear of failure

The sense of emptiness that loss creates is temporary. It also opens doors to the world of opportunities which can give you long-lasting success. Donald Trump, the American business magnate learned a lesson he would never have learnt had he not lost most of his fortune in the nineties. This real estate tycoon faced tremendous challenges in the economy downturn and was on the verge of bankruptcy. His wife had filed for divorce. All

1 Act Two Magazine

these challenges brought the best out of Trump and with some expert business moves, he was able to get out of this and that is what makes Donald Trump great. Steve Jobs, who was ousted from the company he founded, took the loss as an opportunity to build a new life. He founded NeXT and finally, returned to his own company as CEO. Steve Jobs and Donald Trump used their setbacks as opportunities for growth.

Robin Sharma, a renowned motivational speaker, one said, "The thing you resist will persist and the thing you befriend will transcend". He was right. You rise above your fears by looking at them right in the face. You should be willing to take a leap of faith for your dreams.

Failure as Feedback

> *I have not failed. I've just found 10,000 ways that won't work.*
>
> –Thomas Edison

People point each other out as failures. I doubt that is true. How can a human being be called a failure? One may say that a person is strong, weak, thin or fat. However, failure is not an attribute; it is only a circumstance or a situation where the efforts one put in did not reap the expected results. To put the tag 'failure' on someone is to treat him like a commodity.

Human beings can never be products because unlike inanimate things, we can rejuvenate ourselves whenever we feel exhausted.

The greatest pain of humanity is that we have been taught not to fail; more importantly, we have not been taught how to deal with failure. For living a meaningful life, we need to learn how to fail. The only reason we see failed relationships, unencouraging careers, declining health and defeatist individuals is because we do not know how to fail. I firmly believe that the 'how' of a failure is more important than the 'why'. So, once you figure out 'how', you will naturally know why.

Have you observed people who fail once, keep on failing again and again? They keep on following the same path and make the same mistakes while there are other people who fail once and try out different approaches to overcome their failures and emerge with new learning, completely enthusiastic about their failures and full of confidence of achieving something. There is a difference between repeating your mistakes and finding more challenging methods of approaching something you couldn't do the first time.

Learn to fail if you want to succeed

There are many routes to the same place but many believe that there is only one path to success. If they don't get it right the first time, they keep traveling the same path or quit. They keep on trying the wrong way and they simply don't understand that there are other routes which could lead them to their destination.

You become a failure when you tread the same path again and again without learning more about it, without trying out different approaches and without experimenting.

Thomas Edison was experimenting with his light bulb but he failed over and over again. But when Edison was asked if he had failed, he merely said that he had only found 10,000 ways something won't work. He converted his failures into learning. Change the path which doesn't give you results, but always remember the lesson that path taught you; life is all about taking different paths to a destination. One doesn't always need to take the conventional path to reach one's destination. If one of the routes fail you, learn your lesson and move on to the next, try it out and learn your lesson from it. When your learning is complete, you will find the path which will take you to your destination. The key lesson is that each failure is a lesson which equips you with the wisdom that will open the pathway to success sooner or later.

But how do we convert our failures into lessons? We converse with ourselves every moment. When we plan to buy a product, we ask ourselves a number of questions. We wonder if it will help us, or whether it is too expensive or if it has all the features we are likely to need and only then do we take a decision.

We deal with our partners in the same way. We ask ourselves what would be the right time to talk to them and whether they would enjoy going out to dinner more than going to the gadget store next door.

Converting failures to lessons is possible if you ask yourself a specific set of questions.

Instead of saying: "Why this happened to me."
Ask: "How can I use this?" or "What can I learn from this?"

Instead of saying: "I am a failure."
Ask: "What can I learn from it?"

Instead of saying: "I couldn't succeed."
Ask: "How can I succeed in it."

Instead of saying: "I don't know how to do it."
Ask: "From where can I learn and apply to this situation."

All victories are won in the mind first. Convert the ongoing destructive self-criticism into a positive self-appreciation which empowers you instead of bogging you down. Most people who face fears are trapped into negative thinking as they are repeating the same disempowering questions to themselves. Your response depends on the kind of question you ask yourself. A positive question gives you a positive response and a negative question will attract a negative response; thereby trapping you into negative thinking. Ask yourself quality questions and convert your failures into lessons.

Don't Be a Thermometer

You cannot control what happens to you, but you can control your attitude toward what happens to you.

–Brian Tracy

A thermometer shows you the temperature at a particular moment as per the weather. If it's cold, it will drop and if it's hot, temperatures would soar. But you aren't a thermometer! If life gives you warm weather, you don't need to warm yourself accordingly. You have the choice to decide what's best for you.

You are rich – rich in ideas and thoughts that can create a difference

People with a limited income are not as poor as people who have a limited number of options. They are poor because they have not recognized that they have limited choices every moment. The reality is that you have the power to choose the direction you want to go, the road you would like to take and the way you wish to respond. Life's conditions don't make you successful or unsuccessful – You have a choice of experiencing conditions that you're living in, which may not be good but you have a choice in your method of response. It can either be 'Why me' or 'Try me!'

What stops you from becoming the master of your fate and the captain of your soul? The answer is you, the sole creator of yourself. The sum of your present self is nothing but how you responded to life in the past. What you will become depends on how you deal with your life right now; we need to stop being guided by our circumstances. Take control of your destiny.

It is one's head and heart that makes one rich, not money. Just as having no money implies you're broke, having no heart also implies that you're broke, albeit in a different manner. You can get all the money you need when you understand how to use your head and heart in the right measure. Even if you have only ten dollars, but have the head and the heart, come to me, and I will teach you how to enjoy the richness of life. Our heart teaches us to follow our passions and our head teaches us to be intelligent. Both are necessary.

There are two kinds of people: the ones who live according to what their brains tell them and the ones who listen to their hearts. They're normally headed in two different directions. The first group is the better one, they *are* happy and content while the second group only *looks* happy and content. But looking happy doesn't mean feeling happy. It might mean you're feigning happiness. People can look happy on the outside yet feel empty on the inside.

Don't ignore the calling of the heart because only your heart knows your purpose. The head often guards the heart and stops it from exploring. To control your circumstances, develop a skill so your heart can explore the possibilities your life has to offer. Sometimes your head doesn't have all the solutions. It consults the heart too.

Life becomes phenomenal for those who respond tactfully instead of reacting, it becomes lovely for those of you who are cautious and not careless, for those who act and don't wait, and for those who face their lives and do not run away from it. Make your life beautiful by accepting what is happening with utmost willingness and make your present a part of who you are. Your present has been designed that way to give you a chance of personal growth. They are that way to provide you with a chance of personal growth. People escape from one place to another to ignore their past. When a couple breaks up, they tour beer bars individually. When they experience a hard time at work, they hit the smoking lounge. When they experience a loss, they begin taking drugs.

You don't need these external things to change how you feel about life. If you rely on them, you will only experience momentary satisfaction and the next moment you face an internal conflict, you will go back to them for support and end up harming yourself. The real support is inside you – it's called acceptance. Accept your circumstances, accept that you don't have the skills if you do lack them in reality, accept that you can't handle your relationship, accept that you are not worthy of the position you have been given. Accepting reality gives us the power to start again. If you cannot accept things, you cannot move on.

We have two options when we face realities that we often don't want to confront – either we justify our belief and ignore it or we accept it and work on it. We can justify that the world is a mean and nasty place or we can see how we can work to achieve our goals; blaming others is easy but accepting the situation and working on rectifying it is tough. One of my friends broke up with his partner. Not being ready to accept it, he spent three years believing that love is not a good thing, instead of accepting that the relationship didn't work because of his own actions. With acceptance begins the learning process to change ourselves for the better.

Take complete control by accepting your world as it is. Learn to take your destiny in your hands by accepting and responding to life. You will always have a choice in life – justify and ignore it or accept and work it out. Choose the latter!

Expect More

Expect victory and you make victory.

–Preston Bradley

Success is something that you don't pursue, you attract it. Success is not located outside, it's inside of oneself. People believe something will have to happen externally for them to be either rich or happy. They believe they will fall in love when someone comes into their lives. They believe they will start trusting someone when someone else starts trusting them. Everything, actually, starts on the inside.

Everything starts on the inside

There was a man searching for something on the highway under a street lamp for quite a few hours. A policeman at the nearby check post saw this man searching for a long time. He thought of helping him out. The policeman went to the man and asked, "Have you lost something here?" The man replied "Yes, I have lost my keys". The policeman asked if he could help and began to search for the keys with the man. The policeman asked the man to describe how his keys looked so it would be easier to look for them. The man explained how the keys looked and they began to search again. They looked for long without any success. Now, the policeman asked the man where he had seen his keys last. 'In my home,' said the man and began looking again. 'Why are looking for your keys here if you've lost them at home?', asked the policeman, angry and curious. The man replied, 'Because there is no light at my house and there is light here under the lamp'. That's the end of the story, but the end gives us an insight into our own personalities. What we are looking for externally, can be found within ourselves. We only need to switch on the lights to find the keys. The keys to unlocking your potential lies in your mind – just switch on the lights.

You have to learn to love yourself if you want to love others. If you want to trust someone, you must begin to trust yourself. If you want to give respect to someone, you will first learn to respect yourself. Charity begins at home.

Gandhi said, 'You must be the change you wish to see in the world'. Be the change. If you expect more out of your life, begin to expect more from yourself. Expect more from yourself at work, in your relationship, in your social circle and everywhere else. In whatever you do, think how you can put in extra effort to accomplish it.

'Can I give in the extra effort, an extra smile, some extra care, a little extra compassion?'

It all begins with you. When you give more to the world, the world returns to you more than you expect. Exhaust your potential on this planet; this is the best time and the best place.

If you expect to deliver mediocre results, you will never surpass mediocrity. Les Brown said, 'Shoot for the moon. Even if you miss, you'll land among the stars.' Have a standard of excellence in whatever you do and expect more from yourself daily. People say, "I am not getting the results I want in my life". The problem is life gives you returns that are in proportion to what you have given to life so you have to expect more from yourself if you want greater rewards. While running, I realize that if I expect myself to run for two hours, I begin to feel tired after an hour. On the other hand, if I expect myself to run for three hours, I begin to feel tired after two hours. The only thing that changed in the process were my expectations from myself. My performance improved accordingly. It is impossible to build muscles if you don't constantly increase the intensity of your weight training.

When you expect more from yourself, it creates a pressure on yourself to do more, to put in some extra effort. Remember a diamond is nothing but a piece of coal which handled pressure very well. Stress is not always bad. There are two kinds of stress – eustress and distress. Eustress is positive stress. It brings out the best in a person. It happens when you expect or demand more positively from your life in terms of work and relations. You stretch your capabilities beyond your limits to discover a new you. Let your potential shine like a diamond.

People make a great mistake when they expect more from others and less from themselves. They regret the fact that their manager doesn't greet them every day or that their colleagues do not fetch up to give them reports but they forget that people don't act according to someone else's expectations; they act according to their own expectations. Certainty in life is generated not from external circumstances, but from inner circumstances. If you expect more, you can be more and have more of what life has to offer you.

What Do You See

The optimist sees the donut, the pessimist sees the hole.

–Oscar Wilde

What you see around yourself is not as important as how you describe what you see. A few people enjoy looking at a baby and a few get jittery. Different people react differently to babies. Everyone goes through what few variations and vagaries life offers. Our reactions are dependent on our points of view and whether we are inherently positive or negative. From a subjective stance, nothing in this world is either good or bad. We put whatever labels we want to on things.

Sight is important, insight is significant

Labels have a profound effect on our life. Labels affect our emotions and make us lose control of our responses. When people call certain things 'painful', 'difficult' or 'conflicting', they do not understand that their labeling reflects more on themselves than what they are naming. People avoid dealing with negative labels because humans have a tendency to avoid pain and move towards pleasure. When you put a negative label on something, you attach a mental image of pain to the person or the thing and this conditions you to try and escape it.

A good way to see something is to acknowledge it first. Acknowledgement doesn't mean acceptance, it means you know there is a gap which needs to be filled. If you don't feel good about your career, or your relationship, the first step is to acknowledge that there is a gap between your expectations and what you are receiving. People usually avoid the entire issue but avoiding the gap will not fill it nor will it solve the problem. Avoiding doesn't only mean not seeing the existing problem, but also denying it or blaming someone else for it. Acknowledge it if your career is going nowhere, acknowledge it if your friendship is not going very well, acknowledge it if your business is not giving you the returns you expect, acknowledge it if your relationship is not going in the right direction.

Once you acknowledge the gap, it is time to see it with your mind's eye. What is it that you want? What would the situation be like once the gap no longer exists? It can be having a career you like, looking physically fit or acquiring a skill you did not possess previously. There may be a lot of things you want to change about your current situation. It is just like knowing how the road will look like after filling in the potholes.

Once, two people were laying bricks. Someone went to them and asked "What are you doing?" One worker said, "I am laying bricks", and the other worker said, "I am building a beautiful castle". See the castle in your mind before you begin to build it. Be clear in your mind about your outcome and have a blueprint of your expectations. If you don't know the destination, how will you know where to go? Take the leap by defining precisely how you want to see the gap filled up. Your destination decides your direction. If you have a destination, you will know where to start and once you do start, you will know how to continue the journey.

Sight is important, insight is significant. Insight means seeing into the reality of things and not letting yourself be deceived by appearances. Try having an insight into things happening around you. When you know your destination, you will see obstacles and new gaps forming on the way. Don't be distracted on seeing the gaps because they're only waiting to be filled. Legend says there are two wolves inside each of us and they are fighting each other. One wolf makes you see the problems and the other wolf makes you see the solutions. The question is which wolf wins the battle? It is the one you feed. Do you feed the wolf which shows you the problems or the wolf which solves the problems? You have a choice. If you see your career going nowhere, you can either curse your manager and the company or see it as an opportunity to choose a new path. You can see your relationship going nowhere and avoid the situation or you can try to work on the shortcomings of your relationship.

Always remember to keep your sight on the destination. While writing this book, I visualized the book eventually being published. Even during difficult times, when I couldn't find time to complete it, or when ideas weren't occurring to me, the picture of the book in my hand instantly encouraged me. I saw the moment when this book would be in the hands of people and in the bookstores much before I started writing it. Have a picture of your destination in your mind in times of distress. The choice is always yours. Which wolf shall you feed? The one that creates problems or the one that solves them?

What's in this for me?

1. If you resist something, it will persist.

   'Run towards your fear,
   not away from it'

2. Learn to fail if you want to succeed.

   'Failure is a kind of feedback'

3. It is only in your mind that you can be truly rich.

   'Control your attitude'

4. Your external world is a reflection of your internal world.

   'Expect more from yourself'

5. Communicate with yourself.

   'Sight is important,
   insight is significant'

CHAPTER 5

Possibilities

"I was born in obscurity and that is why I am poor," said a man to his friend and his friend replied, "I was born in obscurity and that is why I am rich". Nobody is born in obscurity; it is a condition people create. You can always choose opportunity over difficulty, learning over failure and growth over pain. The choice is ultimately in your hands. Both at home and at work, you are surrounded with possibilities which include building a new career, taking your relationship to the next level, setting up your own business and reaching out to a fresh group of customers. You can change the direction of your life by exploiting the possibilities life has to offer. Neither do you have to drive the same car everyday nor be in a stagnant career simply because you have been doing so in the past. Nothing is permanent and everything is changeable because possibilities are endless.

To create possibilities one has to learn to see the end. Ask "What possibilities do the future hold?" Steven Covey said, "Begin with the end in mind". See the range of possibilities and choose the one that you like best. For your life to change, your choices have to change.

An opportunity is a possibility; it's a door which does not remain open for too long and a shot which might not have any more takes. Once you have lost an opportunity, you will regret it forever so accept it or reject it when it is there. Never regret it after it has gone because it was your choice, after all. Be open to new ideas, information and thoughts, because you never know when one idea can change your life. Flexibility is the name of the game. Be flexible to new approaches of doing things, new skills, new industries that are coming up, new people you are going to meet and all of these are going to add to your life experience.

Someone who does one single thing lifelong will be skilled only in that particular field but a multitasker will always widen his/her perspective and knowledge. Cross-functional knowledge is essential to become the CEO of a company, so it is essential for you to take the right decision and know how the decision will impact the growth of your company.

Ask, Seek, Knock

Ask and it will be given to you; seek and you will find; knock and the door will be opened to you.

–Matthew 7:7

Ask and it will be given to you; seek and you will find; knock and the door will be opened to you.

For everyone who asks, receives; the one who seeks, finds; and to the one who knocks, the door will be opened.' Life is made simpler by these lines from the Bible.

Life has provided you with unlimited possibilities and they are available to those who ask, seek and knock. But somehow people are waiting for something to happen externally to accept the gifts of life. Life can be transformed only when we make a conscious choice. For instance, we need to tell the waiter what we want. Every living moment thus involves making a conscious choice.

Ask and you shall receive
Seek and you shall find
Knock and the door will be opened to you

Everything begins with asking but we are afraid of asking for help, guidance or suggestion because we believe that we will become vulnerable by sharing our weaknesses. Strength comes from overcoming your weaknesses, not from hiding them. If you are facing challenges in your career or your relationship, you should ask for advice from someone who is dealing with a similar situation successfully. You don't have to undergo all the painful experiences to get to the right point, you can learn from what others are doing and change your life instantly. People who do well in their lives usually have a sort of secret recipe and your job is to ask for that recipe and to try and bring in changes in your own life using it. I was talking with a friend who was having a problem selling his company's product. So I asked him if there was anybody who was doing better than him and he said yes, there was someone – a top salesperson of their company who was doing really well. He had befriended the top salesperson of his company who was quite willing to share his ideas with him and were showing results in my friend's career. Asking creates results where action might not. Ask for the right strategy, guidance, coaching and knowledge and that is how the receiving process will begin. Asking is not enough; you also need to seek what you want from life. Set your goals right because they give you direction and focus; people who fail are mostly not sure of what they want from life. All of a sudden, they find out they were either in the wrong relationship or doing the wrong job. So they were just whiling away their time. Having a purpose lends you clarity on what you want from your relationship, career, and social life.

The human mind seeks a goal and in times of conflict, people forget they are spending their energy defending themselves and attacking others while they can collaborate and achieve a win-win situation. Conflicts occur when people shift their focus from achieving what they seek to attacking views others hold. Seeking doesn't mean only setting goals; it also means seeking the right information, new ideas, creative processes and good thoughts. Seek the things which help you in your life and you shall find them, though you will have to search continuously with all your will. Look for positive traits in people and search for joy in your everyday life. You will also find happiness through tough situations and learn through failures only if you look for them. Seek the purpose of life and you shall find it because it begins with you.

St Matthew asks us to ask, seek and knock. Knock on the doors of opportunity; most people fail to recognize an opportunity when they see it and that's all the difference between an unsuccessful person and a successful person. Successful people pounce on opportunities. There are no second takes in life – what you miss, you miss forever. And if you do not find any opportunities, create them.

Legend goes that Alexander the Great was asked if he would occupy the next city if he had the opportunity and he replied, "Opportunity? Why, I don't wait for opportunities, I create opportunities." Do the unexpected and develop a new skill, get new resources, diversify at work, enrich your job with new tasks and do whatever you can to expand your world. You are in control of your destiny and you are the creator of your own life so you can step up and create a new life, a new beginning. Being poor is not something that has happened to you, it is something you have created with your own thoughts but remember you have the opportunity to become rich whenever you want by utilizing opportunities when they present themselves. You don't have to stay at the same place all your life; you can move on and exploit favourable circumstances.

Life is all about asking, seeking and knocking. Keep on asking for the best life has to offer, seek the best in every situation, open the door of opportunity when it presents itself and you will never miss out on the joy life has to offer.

Be Flexible

If you are truly flexible and go until... there is really very little you can't accomplish in your lifetime.

–Anthony Robbins

One should be as fluid and easy as water passing over rocks and creating paths for itself where there are none. Nothing can stop the flow of water; it will flow over every obstacle. And when you put it in a glass, it assumes the shape of the glass, whereas a stone cannot do so. Life gives us challenges in various forms and we have to be as fluid as water when we are tackling these rocks on our path. The art of flexibility is your key to survival. Similarly, you need not stick to the path you have been following; you are free to change your approach.

Rigidity creates a lot more problems than people can imagine; people who think in terms of absolutes have a difficult time coping with changes. They believe there is just about one way of doing everything and block out information that might tell them otherwise. But to improve the quality of your results, you must change your approach.

Be ready for change, be flexible

A straight line on a heart rate monitor means death; the line has to go up and down for the machine to indicate life. There were two friends, a tree and a leaf of grass. The tree grew strong and big, the branches grew too and so did the grass. Once a strong thunderstorm came and the tree was washed away and lying on the ground. But surprisingly the grass was fine and the tree asked the grass how it survived. The grass said, "Because I was moved along with the wind" So, be flexible!

The most hardworking insects are ants and we should learn from them. Whenever you try to stop its way, they will try to move in some other direction but they will just not stop. There might be multitudes of things in your life you might wish to change and you may be working hard towards that. However, in different situations, it would be best to try a new approach. Don't get stuck with one kind of thought; you must have an open mind.

I used to think earlier that the only way to reduce weight was to diet but then someone suggested exercising so I changed my method and started exercising as well. I got better results and I was happy. Later, I realized that meditation was also a way people reduced weight and I tried it. Life involves having to constantly refine your original ideas and methods. A greater number of choices mean a better chance of having the desired results. Being flexible increases your choices, but beware; one must never have too many choices. Often faced with too many options, we fail to act.

Often people say they have no choices left in a particular situation but the reality is that we always hold the choice in our hands; you should realize you have multiple choices to make every day. Poor people operate with very limited choices while the rich have multiple choices at any given point of time. From Bill Gates to Warren Buffet to Carlos Slim Helu–these people have multiple businesses earning them their hefty incomes. People who want to earn a wage have one income resource while people who want to make a fortune, have several.

Variety is the spice of life. Variety comes from new ideas and thoughts. Let new ideas nourish the garden of your mind because you never know how an idea can completely transform your life. Know what leaders did to reach where they are and also look at how people who failed, ended up being successful.

India is a culturally rich country and it is because of the richness of the variety therein that so many different cultures, cuisines and religions can coexist. Life comprises day and night, the four seasons and a wide range of climatic conditions. Variety colors our life and we should acknowledge it.

The 20 Percent

Innovation distinguishes between a leader and a follower.

–Steve Jobs

We all know about the organization which epitomizes innovation in its industry. This is the organization which has woven the world together in a common thread of participating in the quest for knowledge and helped millions of people study subjects ranging from encephalitis to building a spaceship. This organization is Google – the world famous search engine. It is surprising indeed how Google manages to constantly innovate and come up with bigger and better ideas to help their customers. The secret behind their success is definitely their ability to be creative and imaginative – new ideas are always listened to and acted upon. It is the culture of the organization that makes all the difference. They follow a unique concept called the 20 percent work rule, which has helped Google encourage their employees to innovate. According to the 20 percent work rule, the employees spend twenty percent of their office time in taking up initiatives beyond their job descriptions. This motivates the employees to take up projects that are challenging and meritorious, where they tend to execute their best to come up with remarkable product ideas and services. If the project is found relevant they are taken up seriously by the organization.

Do new things

If you want to exploit your creative potential, apply the 20 percent rule in your life and listen to the hidden genius in you; it shall make your innovative abilities clearer. How many of us know how cellophane came into existence? A person sitting at a restaurant saw someone spilling some liquid on a tablecloth. He went back home and thought of how he could come up with a way the tablecloth would not be wet even if liquid were spilled onto it. He came up with the product called cellophane, which is now used extensively in our daily lives. There are infinite possibilities for those who are resourceful and possess vision.

Everything was just a creation of the mind in the beginning. It is only when people with creative minds had the urge to dare and dream, took their ideas to the next level, that their ideas and vision became a reality. However, it is one thing to have ideas but it is quite another to have the skill to execute ideas and make the most of their lives. There are times we think of something and someone converts the thought we had to reality. The difference between you and that person is that he took action and you didn't.

You should write down all your ideas on a sheet of paper after having freed your mind of all past thoughts, thus giving your ideas some free ground. Another reason to write your ideas down is that it is a good way of keeping track of them. The best ideas occur to us in the weirdest of places – Archimedes shouted 'Eureka!' when he discovered that when an object displaces water, the volume of water displaced is equal to the volume of the object; he was in a bathroom. I thought of writing this book when I was driving back home after a tired day at work; I immediately parked my car on the side, grabbed a pen and paper and listed down the chapters I wished to include in this book.

Go beyond your job – it may include preparing sales reports or teaching people but you have to learn to go beyond the limits of prescribed roles and do something unique. You can find a new method of doing your job, or you can go ahead and learn some new aspect of your job; ask yourself if you have done anything new with your area of expertise. If you haven't done anything, get up and do something now. Read a new book, borrow an idea from it, get ideas from your friends or just see if your professors can inspire you. Have a thirst for knowledge: everything you read, listen to and see should enrich you as a person. I like reading and talking to people about their own subjects. I try to add to my knowledge base. What are you doing to expand your knowledge base?

The "I CAN" Principle

Yes, we can.

–Barack Obama, President of the United States of America

There are two kinds of people in the world – people who think they can and people who think they can't and each group tries to consistently influence the other group. Human beings are social and they rely on their ability to influence others as a measurement of their self-worth. You should try and guess for yourself if you're surrounded by people who think they can or by people who think they can't; people who can will challenge you in ways that will benefit you. They will make you push your limits of doing more, being more, having more and living more, whereas people who say they can't will sap your energy by pulling you towards them and making you accept their average standards. They will make you shift your focus onto problems instead of solutions, they will intensify your hurt in difficult situations, disrupt your flow when you are sailing smooth, and they will contaminate your thinking with negative thoughts.

Yes You Can

For the world to progress, we would need more and more active and conscious individuals because they have the potential to solve problems, take up new challenges, fight difficult situations and overcome adversities. People who think they cannot make it will regret the lack they have in life, exist in their past and will hold onto feelings of hurt.

Being faced with the grave challenge of environmental pollution and several deadly diseases because of it, people who think they can't have only one reaction – they let it continue because they're sure nothing can possibly be done about it. The reasons they give vary from lack of capital to scarcity of human labor, from political pressure to systemic issues, from improper planning to failed execution. On the other hand, people who can are trying to effectively tackle the problem: they plant trees, prevent deforestation and use environment-friendly fuel. There are many who do not think they can use social networking sites to bring about a positive change in the world.

Yet, Wael Ghonim, a young computer engineer and Google employee, mobilized millions of Egyptians to hold a peaceful anti-government protest on Facebook. He believed in initiating change and working for it. Some of us believe that the modern woman is too busy with her children to have a really successful and meaningful career.

Yet, Michele Bachmann, a lady with five children, providing foster care for twenty-three teenage girls is a Republican member of the US House of Representatives. She balances work and family life quite well. For everyone who thought banks in America would never survive the financial crisis, Jamie Dimon, current chairman, president and chief executive officer of JP Morgan Chase, one of the Big Four banks of the United States, steered the bank through the global financial meltdown safely yet courageously. When all the other major banks like Bear Stearns, Lehman Brothers, AIG, Countrywide and WaMu were facing difficult times, he believed his bank would survive. He was successful in his mission.

What is more, Barack Obama did not defeat his opponents only with his charisma, the slogan he consistently used during his presidential campaign, "Yes we can" touched the American heart.

Become like one of these people who believe they can do it. Change your focus from:

- Limitations to possibilities
- Necessities to must
- Failures to feedback
- Lose to win
- Impossible to possible
- Lack of resources to resourcefulness

Solve your problems, do not add to them; remember you attract things you focus on in life. Make your mind up about how to solve your problems. Our constant conditioning enforces us to assume we can't. Before you think of solutions, you have to undo all the previous conditioning that you went through. What you think is what you become – the age old formula still works.

A few men and women from all walks of life have proved everyone around them wrong by their attitude. They have consistently focused on the solutions instead of the problem, and instead of thinking why something couldn't be done, they try to figure out a solution.

There is a famous story about two seeds. The first seed said "Wow, I love been planted in the soil where I can spread my roots and open my buds, face the sun and feel the rain on me", while the second seed said, "Oh my God, I don't know what will happen when I put my roots in the dark ground below, what will happen to me when the sun shines and clouds rain." After a few days, the second seed was eaten by a bird because it couldn't grow itself while the first seed grew into a plant and later into a tree, supporting many birds in it. In life you will always have a choice – you can choose to be either of the seeds.

Say Yes to Problems

The problem is not that there are problems. The problem is expecting otherwise and thinking that having problems is a problem.

–Theodore Rubin

The only reason people face problems is because they try to resist them. Observe people around you and you will find that most of them are living in fear and pain because of their inability to accept their problems. Trying to escape your problem or burying it within your unconscious will only persuade it to emerge a while later, stronger than before. Accepting the problem on the other hand, begins the curing process.

Avoiding the problem and blaming others for it are poor strategies; you may choose to ignore a situation at work or just delay a confrontation with your child for something inappropriate he may have done. You may also avoid addressing some health problems you have. In all these situations you are avoiding the problem, which is a short-term strategy for reducing your pain and one which may ultimately be dangerous. Your health may deteriorate beyond cure, your child may do something seriously wrong

Don't React
Simply Respond

and you may find yourself not being able to deliver as well as you ought to at work. Blaming is worse because it means shifting the entire responsibility of the situation elsewhere. You have to take complete responsibility of what you are and what you have done.

Martin Kitch was a software professional from California and a happily-married man with two kids. One fine day, his wife began arguing about how she expected him to help her with her daily chores and Martin decided to take a quick vacation. When the same thing recurred after his vacation, he escaped to his office. One day he came home from office only to discover a letter which said – "I am leaving you because I always wanted to talk about our relationship and what we were expecting from each other, but you always tried to run away from the situation. We failed to understand each other. Take your medicines regularly, take care. I will call you tomorrow about our divorce proceedings. Yours truly, Suzanne." And Martin was devastated! There was nowhere for him to run to now. The only people without problems are the dead. Sometimes people bury their problems but the problems return bigger and perhaps more threatening. A teenaged drug addict was once diagnosed with high blood pressure and other cardiovascular problems. He left drugs after undergoing treatment at a rehab facility but ignored his high blood pressure.He simply buried the problem and went on with life. He started working at a good multinational organization where the work pressure he faced daily took a toll on his health. One day while driving, he felt an excruciating pain in his chest and was rushed to the nearest hospital and the doctor said he had a heart attack. He could not survive the second attack which he had subsequently. The problem he had buried within him took his life. Accept your problem and find out what can you learn from it because resistance only creates pain; the more you resist a problem, the more you suffer. Every problem is an opportunity to grow and learn something new. Martin could have grown as an individual and forged a greater bonding with his wife, while the young boy would have learned to balance his work and his health.

People who live unbalanced lives focus more on external events rather than concentrating on themselves. Ignore your high blood pressure and you may have to face a cardiac malfunction or miss several deadlines at work and risk losing your job. Situations worsen when one ignores present problems and lives a reactive life. Living a life of reaction is easy but painful because you're never in control; you're always stuck in situations which are controlling you. The word is 'reaction' because your behaviors and actions are shaped by the events happening around you; most people live this way and handle their presents without a thought about their futures.

While choosing a career for oneself or getting a job, students get into the reactionary mode and accept the first job they are offered. They're reacting to momentary excitement and peer pressure and taking up jobs which are clearly not good enough for them; their placement becomes a sort of misplacement, actually. This is an example of being reactive.

Don't behave like the ostrich, which has the peculiar quality of hiding its head in the sand when it sees an enemy coming towards it; it assumes the enemy will not be able to see it if it hides its face. She adopts the reactive method of living and acts only when the enemy has reached her. Life implies a bunch of unexpected situations where it's always better to be proactive and either to prevent the problem from occurring at all or reducing the impact of the problem by taking action instantly. This gives you the power to live life on your own terms. Winners are proactive because they know how to respond correctly; they notice the symptoms of high blood pressure and take medicine for it and they never miss their deadlines. They are always in control of every situation life creates for them. We become proactive when we examine our interests and inclinations before taking the first job which we are offered and take care of our children before they take care of us. They decide on their future aspirations before moving to a different company and spend enough time in a relationship before taking it to the next level. There are many ways to begin.

Resistance is an obstacle you have to cross when you're being proactive; you have to consciously take charge of yourself. If you're facing relationship trouble, call up your partner and talk about it. Likewise, if you're having weight issues, then join the local gym. There are many possible solutions to a certain situation, but the first step towards resolving anything is being consciously responsible and active while dealing with a problem. By denying that you have a problem,you are only resisting it and giving the problem a chance to grow and get the better of you. Always accept problems as opportunities for you to grow and learn. Accepting the problem begins the process of resolving the problem. Resistance creates stress, which in turn can damage you emotionally. Carrying a bag of trouble on your way to fame and glory will only slow you down. Acceptance can make that bag lighter.

What's in this for me?

1. Ask for wisdom, seek the right answers, knock on the doors of opportunity.

   'Ask, seek and knock'

2. Don't just keep knocking the doors, sometimes you have to create a new door.

   'Be flexible in your approaches'

3. There are endless possibilities in life.

   'Do new things!'

4. Challenge yourself daily by becoming a person who believes in himself/herself!

   'Yes you can!'

5. Be proactive and responsible for yourself.

   'Face your problems,
   don't escape them'

CHAPTER 6

Practice

You become what you practice all day long. Practice creates patterns in the mind. You can choose to create patterns of success or patterns of failure. Everything depends on what you practice every day. You have to practice being better than what you are, you have to practice high thinking and you also have to practice acting on your ideas. Practice your polished skills and also work on acquiring a new one. If you keep on practicing the right way, you will keep on getting better results. The price of success is practice. No one in this world has been able to master a profession without practice. Even a natural talent needs practice to refine it. From the likes of Sachin Tendulkar to Michael Jordan to Beethoven to Picasso, practice has made them icons in their own fields. Sharpen your talent by practicing and working hard on yourself. If you work hard on yourself, life will be easy on you and if you don't work on yourself that much, life will be hard.

You need to practice physically, mentally and emotionally. Use your power of visualization to practice better. Scientists have proved that a visual motor rehearsal or visualization can improve the performance of athletes greatly. When you visualize, you create a blueprint of your performance in your mind before the actual action. The blueprint helps you fine-tune your actions when you act in reality. But visualization alone may not work for many. Therefore it is essential to spice up your visualization with emotional intensity. Emotions create the difference between ordinary and extraordinary performances.

You must take massive mental, emotional and physical actions to create momentum for success in life. Take action in your mind by painting picture of the kind of life you wish to design for yourself, have that picture all the time in your mind. We have never learned to fail, and that is also an art. When you fail, don't face the ground. Face up towards the blue sky. And when you look at the blue sky and the sun shining, you will be motivated to rise again. When you face tough situations in life, learn to the see the best picture in your mind of what you want. Do things with passion and energy because when you have the energy, you can produce massive results at work. High-energy people always pep up the moods of people around them. Everyone wants to be surrounded by people who can lift up their moods. Become an energy-producing machine. I read a signboard at one of the cafes in Delhi that said "Do it with passion or don't do it at all". All dispirited action produces dispirited results! Don't just stop there!

Instead, act positively. Pick up the bricks and start building the castle. A blueprint in the mind won't move a single brick from the ground. You must act by picking up the bricks and putting them in the right order in your blueprint. Action precedes results. Act and you shall achieve!

Use What You Have

Miracles happen every day, change your perception of what a miracle is and you'll see them all around you.

–Jon Bon Jovi, singer

You don't need a million dollars to succeed

Voltaire, a French author and philosopher said, "Life is like a game of cards. Each player must accept the card life deals him or her. But once they are in hand, he or she alone must decide how to play in order to win the game." What are people doing today? They are more concerned about what others have than they are with their own cards. They are more willing to find out about others' lives and see what cards they have. They have reference points in people around them, instead of focusing on what they have. They compare their standards with the standards of people around them and are more interested in the car their neighbors have than in their own children; and more concerned about the progress of their colleagues than in their own progress. People are more worried and curious about how much money others are making than they are about their own bank balance. They're happy if someone makes a little less than them. And when someone makes more, they try and pacify themselves. Have your own standards, stop looking at others' cards around you; focus instead on the cards you have. People say, "Tell us whether the glass is half full or half empty". I say "Be thankful that you have a glass and there is water in it". Don't compare yourself with others, compare yourself with the one person you should always try to outdo – the person you were in the past. Become better than you were yesterday, compete with yourself and ask yourself everyday, "What can I do today to become better than yesterday?" You can do so much more when you compete with yourself and raise your bar every time. When you compete with people around you, you restrict your growth to the level of growth others can achieve. Compete only with yourself.

Doom strikes when a player begins to think that others have a better hand than him. With this belief, people begin to sell themselves short. They believe neither in their talents nor in themselves. People in this way, deny themselves the assignment they had been waiting for and the increment they deserve. They might never propose to the person of their dreams for fear of being rejected. At home, they deprive themselves of the love that they so deserve. One must value oneself for what one is truly worth and then live up to the expectations set by him or her. Go and grab the assignment that comes your way even if you don't believe in yourself.

Martin Luther King Jr. said it right – "Faith is taking the first step even when you can't see the whole staircase." Have faith in your ability to make it through. Ask for the increment that you deserve, approach the person you love, stand up when you need to stand up for yourself. Everyone loves people who believe in themselves. Faith means knowing that the cards you have will help you win the game. It makes you certain in life situations.

Let us suppose I ask you to move from one corner of your living room to the opposite even when there is no light, you will certainly go where I want you to go without banging into things. It is because you're so well-accustomed to the room that you know where everything is. Your mind carries a perfect picture of the room and your mind guides you. It is because you have an image in your mind and you step forward with faith in accordance to the image. But the image *has* to be there. See yourself winning the game of life with the cards life has given you; see how you can use the cards to win. Faith precedes performance. Without faith, you cannot peak. Maxwell Maltz, author of the best seller *Psycho-Cybernetics, A New Way to Get More Living Out of Life* says that "self-image" is the key to human personality and human behavior.

Change your image and you change your personality and your behavior. Work on yourself and everything would be taken care of. Life does not employ you, you employ life. You take your decisions. You plan your investments; how you want your personal corporation to grow and what elements you want eliminated. You are your own brand ambassador. Focus on developing skills and talents by learning and reading. Take conscious control of your organization; allow consultants to help you but take your own decisions. Don't let the consultants or friends talk you into something you don't want. Time is your most precious resource, money can be recovered but not time. Use time as a resource to develop your self-esteem. The confidence of an organization grows as does the quality and the originality of its products. Develop unique skills and talents by exploring new areas, meeting new people and reading subjects beyond your area. Your self-esteem is directly proportional to the time you invest in your own development.

But how is one to win the game of cards? Every person in the world is unique. They have different skills, talents and potential. They stay in different environments and react differently. To compare yourself with them would be like comparing apples with oranges. Instead, appreciate your beauty. Count your assets and liabilities mentally. Know what your strengths are – they may be a certain special talent, your shining personality or your communication skills. Your liabilities could be not having a particular skill you require, being stuck in the wrong job or not being able to deliver at your workplace. Understand all the elements well and start working on them. Invest more time and energy in whatever is your drawback. Don't forget – you own your life, you take your own decisions.

But the question still remains. How can you win? And the answer is, the man with the best hand might not always win, but the man who knows how to play his cards right always does.

Practice Makes You Perfect

An ounce of practice is worth more than tons of preaching.

–Mahatma Gandhi

Practice makes a man perfect. That's something we have heard a lot from our elders. Following this advice, I had begun learning how to drive a car. I knew if I practiced enough, I would be able to drive it smoothly. Though I did drive smooth eventually, I paid quite heavily for it too. I kept the car in the lower gear for far too long. That's how I thought cars were driven! That's how I kept practicing! And I believed practice made a man perfect. And later, my car broke down because of the way I had been practicing. I had to spend quite heavily on repairing it. I later learnt how to drive fast even on a low gear. I also **learnt** that it is only the correct kind of practice that can make a man perfect. If you keep on doing the wrong things, how can you be on the right track? You have to be rightly informed to be on the right track.

Perfect practice makes a man or a woman perfect

Our brain contains millions of neurons which are connected together. They are set on fire whenever you think or do something. Initially, when you perform an action, certain sets of neurons are fired in your brain. It is like an electric impulse flowing through a few sets of neurons. If you repeat the act, the same set of neurons will be fired. No matter how many times you do it, the same set of neurons will be fired. What happens next is these neurons begin to bond. The neurons which fire together wire together. Excellence in performance comes from the wiring of such neurons. It happens when you don't have to think while performing an act, when you can afford to be effortless and smooth. Your mind just obeys your command and a known set of neurons are fired.

So if you wish to master any area of your life, get the right information, and keep on practicing again and again, until it becomes a cakewalk for you. Participants often ask me how I am able to impart so much information with so much energy within such a limited amount of time during my training programs. And my answer is, "Because I have been doing all these seminars for so long". There is no secret to achieving perfection. The key here is to deliver excellence through the art of intelligent repetition.

Ever learned to ride a bicycle? If you cannot maintain balance or maneuver through tricky roads or even use the accelerator and brake properly, then you just haven't learnt to ride a bicycle. One never knows how many skills may be required to handle a bicycle properly. According to one of the most widely used learning models called Conscious Competence model, there are certain stages in the process of developing competence. The first stage is called Unconscious Incompetence, where you don't know what you don't know. You don't know that you need to acquire a specific set of skills to ride a bicycle. So someone tells you about the skills you need to acquire, and you become aware of it. You become aware that you don't have the skills to ride a bicycle. This stage is called Conscious Incompetence, where you are conscious of things that you don't know or have. So you begin to practice.

You pick your first bicycle and get on it. You are conscious of your hand and feet coordination, you are conscious of how you are going to press the brake, the pace at which you have to paddle, the way you are going to make a turn. This stage is called Conscious Competence. You are consciously involved in practicing the skill. But to master it, this needs to be an involuntary act. This can only happen through regular practice. The more you practice the skill, the better the neurons in your brain will be fired. The less, therefore, will you have to think about your performance. So the more you ride your bicycle, the better you will be at riding it. This stage is called Unconscious Competence, where you are not required to worry about your performance. It becomes a way of life for you.

What's in it for you? To become a master, you need to know what skills you lack and what you need to do about it. Once you know what you have to change about your life, you become conscious of your incompetence. Sometimes people cannot accept the reasons for their unhappiness. They keep justifying their life to themselves and others. So finding out what needs to be changed is the first step. You may say, "Nishit, I am leading the perfect life, I don't think there is any need to change".

It is really good if you are leading a good life and I think it's the exact reason you should perhaps try to change yourself for the better. Anything that doesn't grow dies. Take your career to the next level, upgrade your skills to a level no one has done before, and create a standard that will amaze people around you. There are no limits to how much human potential can increase and improve. It is a continuous process. After that, it's time to practice. Hit the floor, go to the gym, open your books, attend a training session, get a coach or do whatever you can to get rid of your incompetence and rise to the next level. Keep up your efforts until you acquire the competence you need to master the area you were weak in. Practice correctly.

In his book *Outliers – The Story of Success*, Malcolm Gladwell explains the 10,000 hour rule. To master your craft, you must practice for 10,000 hours. Picasso was once asked by a woman to paint her. Picasso agreed and with just one stroke, the painting was begun and completed. The woman was amazed by the work. He then said, "That will cost you $5000" The women was taken aback by the price and she replied, "But it took you only a few seconds to make it" Picasso, on hearing it, said, "It took me all my life". Practice precedes excellence.

Take Action

Action is the foundational key to all success.

–Pablo Picasso

Thinking is just the first step in your way to success. You need to think before you act. Napolean Hill was correct when he thought of the title of his most popular book, *Think and Grow Rich*. He believed thinking was an essential element while making your fortune. Some people have obviously understood it to mean that thinking is the most important thing but that is wrong. No idea is worth anything if it is not executed. Right from Edison to

Thought in action is the most powerful energy source

Bill Gates, people have had to execute their ideas. So let me rephrase Hill's words and say 'Ideate, Work and Commit Yourself to Growing Rich.' Not everyone who knows the answer raises their hand when they're actually asked the question in class. And all of them would regret it later. You may know so many things in life, but that is not a guarantee that you will succeed. Knowing doesn't lead you to success, it is *knowing* and *doing* combined, which give you results. You may know that your life has to change, but until you act, nothing will happen. You may know that your relationship is going nowhere, but just knowing that won't change the status of your relationship. You may know you're not doing the right job but somehow they don't know that they must act to change their life's circumstances.

With action you give a new direction to the journey of your life. If you do not like your present circumstances, simply change your course of thought and action. Direction affects your destination so if you don't like your current life's circumstances, simply take action and change your course. A ship will keep on moving in the same direction if the captain doesn't order his men to steer it towards a new direction. Steering it five inches away might actually change its destination. Small bits and pieces add up to huge successes. Action produces the momentum for a long-term change. Everyday, commit to an action you would like to take to improve your life and you will land up in a different zone all together in a year. You don't have to live life the same way all throughout, you have a choice to take action and change a little everyday and your destination would automatically change.

But people leave it all to God. 'God helps so many people and so He will help me too'. There was a man who was very religious and had faith in the Almighty. He would perform all kinds of rituals to please God. And on seeing this, God was very happy. One fine day, the city was flooded and the man was stuck within his home. And he prayed to God to help him. While he was praying, a boat came by and asked him to jump on. The man said, "No, God will come to pick me up, let me pray." And the boat went away. The water level began to rise so he climbed on the roof. This time around a helicopter came by and asked him to catch the rope so that he could be lifted onto it. The man said, again, "God is there to help me; he will come to my rescue." And again he refused. Soon the water level rose and he was caught in the current and was drowned. He passed away. Because he was a follower of God, his soul got a chance to meet God.

He was angry when he met God and asked him "Is this the fate of the man who followed you every moment of his life? Couldn't you come and save me?" God replied, "Child, I had sent you the boat and the helicopter to save your life, but you turned away what I had sent." The soul was perplexed. He had learnt his lesson. The lesson is that even God helps those who help themselves. There are certain things in life which we can't understand. You must involve yourself in the process to understand your progress. Confucius once said, "I hear and I forget. I see and I remember. I do and I understand." Doing starts the learning process because you understand the process by being part of the process.

There are two approaches to life – decide or delay. You take a decision but delay the execution of that decision. For example, someone says, "I would like to start jogging from tomorrow", and the tomorrow never comes, or "I am going to take my kids on a vacation next week", the next week never comes. This is not a healthy approach because you procrastinate. Procrastination has been the most common cause of regret in life. And then there is the other approach – decide and deliver. You make a decision and then immediately take action. You gain momentum and make progress even though it is only a little step forward. Little actions add up to give you noteworthy successes.

Acting after your time is over, creates regret. At times if you miss the train, you will be reminded of it forever and harp on it – that the train was there, the weather was good, there were plenty of good seats. The door was right in front of you, *but* you didn't get through the door. Taking action is difficult, but you know what is even more painful – regret. The pain of regret is always more than the pain of taking action. Take action now!

Power of Persistence

> *I do the very best I know how – the very best I can; and I mean to keep on doing so until the end.*
>
> –Abraham Lincoln

Everyone would know a young chap who had once lost his job at a very young age, a few people to guide him, he tried to set up a business but it didn't work well, he had been defeated many times in state and other legislative elections, but he still persisted towards his goal, he had a nervous breakdown and some very tough personal moments but he didn't allow any of this to stop him. He knew no one could stop him from being resilient and trying to make it on his own. And ultimately after a series of setbacks, he became the President of the United States. His name is as popular as were his oratorical skills. He has always been an example of courage and persistence. The man was Abraham Lincoln.

A gardener knows how to nurture his farm. He waters the plants, weeds, the adjoining grounds regularly and fertilizes the soil. If, at all, he stops these tasks, the plant stands the risk of being destroyed. Everything does not have instant results. It might take some time but with perseverance and persistence, there will be long-term results. Keep on putting the water of your efforts on the plant of your dreams regularly, and one day you will get the fruit you had longed for – as you sow so shall you reap.

Persist like an ant take action like a lion

Persistence is a mixture of multiple ingredients–

1. Emotional Intensity: Your ability to direct all your emotional force into a certain path makes a huge difference. There are a few people who destroy themselves completely after something bad befalls them. On the other hand, there are people who treat the painful event as an instigation to do better in their lives. A boy named Nick Vujicic has guided his emotions with such tremendous will power that he stands as an example of an extreme amount of

self-motivation. He was born with no arms and no legs in a society where it becomes difficult to survive if you even look physically different. He guided his emotions and decided to direct all his energies in fulfilling his desire of helping people live better lives. He guided his psychological pain towards his ambition and now he is a successful motivational speaker and a celebrated author. Direct your emotions in the direction where you want to go. Don't resist any emotion, but guide it so that it helps you and does not stop it.

Your emotional intensity is the–

- fire which melts even the toughest metal
- force which can create miracles in your life
- storm which can become a tornado

2. Clarity of Direction: Do you have a clear view of where you are headed? Have you even decided where to direct your emotions? Undirected emotions can be a cause of disease, both mental and physical. Accumulated emotion may become a tumor, a group of dead cells. These emotions may cause severe problems if not directed towards the right end. Even the scientific community now believes that the cause of physical disease is rooted in emotional troubles people face. I recall meeting

someone at a training session, who said she had gone to an oculist for a pain she had in her eye. He asked her to let go of whatever stress she was facing on a daily basis. So she took up tennis as a hobby and now she has directed all her stress and negative emotions into the game of tennis. Along with that she has also gained public recognition on her skills at playing tennis. Did she stop there? No. She is now a state player and has given up banking to take up tennis coaching.

3. Importance of the goal: Is your outcome significant to you? Answer these questions and check with yourself: Shall I rejoice when I have attained the outcome? Will I be willing to take out time to achieve the outcome? Will it be useful for me as an individual? Are the benefits more than the efforts I will have to put in? Does the outcome benefit the people who are connected to me in any way? If the answer to every question is 'yes', you are on the right track and the goal is important to you. Sometimes we begin by investing a lot of effort in pursuing something and then we lose interest in it. Sustainability becomes a problem. Do you recall the last time you joined the gym and then after two or three months you found it difficult to keep your spirits as high as they had been when you joined? But I know of people whose day is incomplete

without their daily trip to the gym. Know the importance of your goal; if your goal is not important, then chances of you following it are dim.

4. Plan your journey: Failing to plan is planning to fail. No plan means no direction, which means no action. It results in an accumulation of emotions, or directing those emotions in the wrong channels. You would not like to bury your money underneath the ground to rot nor would you like to purchase products which you don't need. Your emotions are like your money and they need to be utilized in way that is beneficial for you as well as others. Plan out a way you will direct these emotions.

How would you guide an:

Emotion of disgust – begin to trust people.
Emotion of disappointment – by being optimistic.
Emotion of remorse – by showering someone with your love.

Find the right channel to guide your emotions consistently. This would keep you motivated to work for your outcome.

Being persistent can help you develop your self-esteem and will power. The more persistent you are, the more chances you have of developing your internal strength.

Use these ingredients to become successful: (1) Develop emotional intensity (2) Clarity in direction (3) Know the importance of your goal and (4) Plan your journey

Power of Decisions

> *Once you make a decision, the universe conspires to make it happen.*
>
> –Ralph Waldo Emerson

In the corporate arena, what differentiates one level of hierarchy from the other? It's the ability to take effective decisions. The more effective your decisions are at work, the better are your chances of being promoted. It is the decision-making skill that people have that decides the progress of the company. The secret to a happy marriage is having taken a good decision at the right time and the reason for successful business ventures are also good decisions. And a good decision comes from having thought out the entire thing from the beginning. But do we actually know how to take the right decision? It is a relevant topic but we never hear of it being taught in schools and colleges. They don't teach students how to take the correct decision even though they know students will have to take some tough decisions

Be conscious and take decisions all the time

after their studies are over. There are so many career options after graduation! Which do you take up and which do you pass over? One wrong decision and you might just have to pay a heavy price! Effective decisions are what father success.

You need to work hard daily to develop your decision-making skills. You need to start taking decisions regularly in all areas of your life, be it emotional, social, physical, intellectual or anything else. Instead of letting life happen to you, you need to decide what you want life to be. Start by taking smaller decisions and act on them. This will develop your self esteem. You will feel confident. A friend was troubled because of her weight and her self-esteem was quite low. But when I saw her a few months back, she had changed completely, she was now living a fulfilled life with perfect health and high self-esteem. I asked the secret and she said, "It all started by deciding to go for a ten-minute walk". And I was surprised! How can a ten-minute walk change the entire life? She shared the story of her transformation with me; it had been no big deal for her to go on a ten-minute walk. But then she gradually increased the time to twenty minutes. And then, to forty minutes. And then, two hours. She started with a small decision and with every win she developed the self-esteem to do more for herself.

But how is someone to take the right decision? There are people who take lots of decisions, but they are still stuck at the same place. You need to know the psychology of effective decision-making; better decisions are a direct result of the experience life gives you. If you want to take better decisions, you need to learn to borrow. Borrow information and knowledge from your past experiences and from the people who have already trodden the path which you are now travelling. You may initially be too young to refer to the wealth of experience that I am referring to and in this stage, you may take a lot of wrong decisions. This will add to your experience, but once you take the same decision after a while, it would be called foolishness. Growth is the order of the day, so if not in terms of time, try and grow in terms of the experience you have collected. A bad decision today can lead you to a wise decision tomorrow, only if you learn from it.

You may think you're living a comfortable life and you do not wish to take a decision at all. Now, the answer to this dilemma would also be a decision in itself. If you don't make a decision then you may have to suffer the consequences of it because every effect has a cause. Your indecisiveness may land you in an unpleasant situation, so why do we not take control of our own lives and initiate a better cause by deciding how we want to live our lives? If you don't make a decision for yourself, some other person would do it for you and it may not be what you want for yourself at all. Your present life conditions are a reflection of the decisions you made in the past, so if you want to change your tomorrow it's time to make decisions about how you want to live your life. You had set a cause in motion in the past which is giving you the effect today.

Decide on:

What new skills would you like to work on in the next two months?
What kind of a relationship you like to have with your partner?
What kind of a financial situation do you foresee for yourself?
Which activity fulfills you the most?
What markets will you focus on in the next quarter?

One should not just live life randomly or accept life's conditions because you are not a thermometer. You can take control of your tomorrow by deciding how you like your life to unfold today. Make as many decisions as possible and live up to them. Anthony Robbins, the world's most renowned motivational speaker gets it right when he says, "Success in life is the result of good judgment. Good judgment is usually the result of experience. Experience is usually the result of bad judgment." Even if your decisions are not correct, know that you are learning and adding to your wealth of experience. Once you decide on something, remove all possibilities of going back, burn your bridges and you will reap the harvest.

What's in this for me?

1. Without faith, you don't experience peak performance.

   'Faith precedes performance'

2. Perfect practice makes a man perfect.

   'Unconscious competence is mastery'

3. Knowing and doing together give you results.

   'Thought plus action
   equals results'

4. Persist like an ant and take action like a lion.

   'The power of persistence
   always works'

5. Effective decisions father success.

   'Decide where you want
   your life to stand'

CHAPTER 7

Potential

The greatest question in human history is "Who are you?"

It's the question that has intrigued even the greatest minds. The answer is yet to be found! The next great question is "What lies within you?" What lies within you is unlimited potential. Legend says that when the earth was formed, everyone had magical powers. They had powers to change shapes and to have anything they desired. But people began to misuse the power they got. So God hid all magical powers in an undiscoverable place. He thought of hiding them on the mountains and in the forests but he decided otherwise. Humans were amazing creatures; they would discover where the hidden powers were. So God decided to hide all the magical powers within the heart of the human. Humans would look outside forever; they would never look within themselves to find out what was within.

Your power lies inside you, not outside. Stop your search for happiness, knowledge, love, respect and care. Everything is available within you. The only thing you need to do is light the switch. Fire your unlimited potential. Your potential is like a sleeping giant which needs to wake up. Wake this sleeping giant up. There are two ways of waking it up. It can wake on its own through the massive pain of the needle. It is the needle of pain which jolts the human from the outside. Sometimes your greatest pain releases your hidden potential. People who go through difficult circumstances become the masters of their lives, like charcoal turns into diamond under tremendous pressure. Human beings shine when they handle the pressure they're intended to handle. It is noticeable how most motivational speakers are the ones who undergo a phase of struggle pretty early in their lives in some manner. Trying to change their circumstances, they discover their true potential lies in lending people a helping hand. They help people around them and in turn help themselves.

Don't let your emotions lie dormant. You never know how small a thing can transform your life. Sometimes a story or an intense conversation or a TV program or a movie may change your worldview. Expose yourself to life; do not hide behind the curtains you have made for yourself. Life is truly beautiful for those who know how to experience it in the right way. It's your time, make it big, make a difference and create history.

Make a Ding

I want to make a ding in the universe.

–Steve Jobs

Steve Jobs. Whatever you may say to describe him, he makes a difference because he made his presence felt in the world in every way possible. Had he been alive, I think this is what he would have said, "I never worked in my life, I did what I love to do so that I could leave a legacy behind". He created things which would outlast his existence. He was the originator of the technical revolution through his own brand Apple, creating products like iPhone, iPod and Macintosh which changed the way people used technology. He did his part of the work in this world, and it is time for you to recognize your part and play your role in the functioning of the universe too.

You don't need to be an innovator (though you can be one) and start following Steve's path. Try creating your own path instead. Steve successfully made a ding in the universe. Have you figured out how you are going to make a ding?

It doesn't matter what you are doing, unless you are doing something and contributing to the world in some way. There is no work which is small or big in this world. Every little bit is a contribution to our planet and big in its own way. In the context of organizational skills, you will find that both leaders and followers are needed. For truly, of what use is one without the other? Every task is essential in this world and the only thing that matters is the attitude with which you perceive it.

Move the world with your work

Sir Martin Luther King Jr. said,

"If a man is called to be a street sweeper, he should sweep streets even as Michelangelo painted, or Beethoven composed music, or Shakespeare wrote poetry. He should sweep streets so well that all the hosts of heaven and earth will pause to say, here lived a great street sweeper who did his job well."

Identify how your work is contributing to the society, how it is making a difference in the lives of people. If you are a software engineer, then understand how you are making people's live easier and more comfortable when you create the software they will use. If you're a student, realize you are a tiny part of what we call the literacy rate in our country. If you're a salesman, understand you are helping people buy what they need to make their lives simpler. If you're an accountant, you're making it easier for people to manage their finances right. There is a direct connection between the outcome of your work and the way in which it will benefit society. Identify and understand this connection. Knowing what you are doing is *worthwhile* and, in a way, affecting someone in a positive way is the greatest motivation for people. So many people do not work hard enough because they're not sure how their work makes a difference to the organization or, on a greater scale, to the rest of society. People need to feel that their work is important and is contributing to the greater good of society and they want to know how exactly they are doing it.

Doing worthwhile work is not only applicable to your workplace, but in every aspect of your life. You can make a ding in all aspects of your life. You are playing so many roles in your life. For your employer, you may be a salesperson or an executive or a human resource professional, but for your family you may be a father or a mother or a daughter or a brother or a lover, and for your friend you may an associate or a support or simply a friend. Play all these roles with compassion and energy. You can make a ding as a daughter by making your family proud of yourself, you can make a ding as a friend by providing emotional support to your friend, you can make a ding as a lover by hugging or kissing your spouse and showing your love for them.

The problem is when we cannot understand whether at all our efforts are affecting people's lives in a positive way. Sometimes people won't give you immediate feedback on your efforts. You may not get to know how you are contributing. Hence you need to consciously convince yourself of your contribution. Let's start with this exercise:

Fill this up and pin it to your notice board or somewhere beside your bathroom mirror: I am __________ and I am making a ding in the universe by _________

E.g. I am a motivational speaker, a trainer and an author and I am making a ding in the universe by assisting people live empowered lives through my books and trainings sessions

I am a salesperson and a good communicator and I am making a ding in the universe by making my customers happy and satisfying their needs.

I am a reservation executive and I am making a ding in the universe by having a friendly relation with my customers and planning vacations for them, thereby helping them stay happy.

I am a father or a mother and I am making a ding in this universe by helping my children and being with them every single moment of our lives. Look at this everyday to remind yourself of what your position in your workplace or your family is and how you contribute to everyone's lives and eventually make it better. When people don't get any feedback, they tend to lose motivation. This leads to an assumption that either they are not needed or their work is not adding value in any way.

Don't let people fall in this trap. Try and convince them of the important of the work they do. Tell them specifically how their actions affect people around them. Let your boss know how his public appreciation of your work keeps you going all year long and express how happy you feel when a friend texts you, asking you about your health and happiness.

Attitude of Gratitude

I was sad because I had no shoes until I met a man that had no feet.

–Anonymous

Thank yourself for every gift that has been presented to you in your life. Most people do not live in the present, which is where they belong. They depend on some external event to occur which will make them happy. They wait for the new car or the much-awaited promotion to feel blessed and happy. These people are the ones who live in the future, without savoring the gifts of the present. They forget to live today because they have been putting off their present to a distant future which may or may not happen. Why? Why not remind yourself of all the tiny ways in which you are blessed? Remind yourself of all the people who make your life amazing, all your material comforts and your health, for which you should thank the deity you believe in.

Gratitude gives birth to energy

Thank everyone you are grateful to right now. You shall not only feel good about yourself. You will also be reminded of the thousand blessings you forget to count every day. These blessings are what your life is all about. Thank your parents who gave you your life, made the right choices for you. Thank your friends for having supported you when you were in trouble. Thank your mentors who guided you with their wisdom. Thank also the people who hurt you for it is due to them that you grew in emotional strength and maturity. Do not forget to thank God for having made you the wonderful person that you are. In certain moments of our life, we lose focus of what is right. We mull over things we have no control over and this eventually disempowers us. We may be thinking of how a certain relationship failed or how we had a bad day at work. We keep thinking the same thing over and over again. So we're not really having a bad time. We're choosing to focus on the wrong things of our life, thereby picturing our present to be worse than it is. At that moment we need to shift our focus immediately to something which will make us happy and ecstatic. We have all the answers and solutions inside us and the only thing that will take them out is to shift our focus towards them.

There was a boxer who was a world champion fighting for his title in the final match. The opponent was a very tough competitor and pounding the champion with heavy blows in each round. But the coach knew what was going wrong. He went to the champion in the break and motivated him with glorious speeches on how he had won in the past and asked him to thank the Almighty for whatever he had won. He also reminded the champion, how he used to feel when he had won three continuous championship tournaments in the past. The champion felt a surge of energy at that point of time and went to the ring, and defeated his opponent. There was no change in his strategy or his fighting style, the only thing that had changed was his focus. When he was focusing on how strong his opponent was, he began to lose, but as soon he shifted his focus to his past strengths and thanked God, he unleashed the real champion inside him and won. Remind yourself of the past positive experiences of your life and thank God for making you who you are.

Start afresh, start today. Go and thank all the people who have contributed to your life. Without them you would have never been who you are. Say thank you to your friends who supported you in times of despair, say thank you to your family for being there for you when you were alone, say thank you to your neighbor who gave you food when no one was at home, say thank you to your teachers who guided you on the path of your destiny, say thank you to strangers who influenced your life in the minutest way. More importantly, thank the people who only pretended to be your friends and might have deliberately harmed you behind your back. They made you grow as an individual. Thank those people who left you alone when you needed them, they unleashed the power within you. That's courage in action. Without courage you don't enjoy life with all its flavours. Be bold but, more importantly, be thankful.

There is a ritual which helped me a lot while I was writing this book. I call it the 'Twenty Minutes of Gratitude'. I practice it thrice a week and it has given to me a greater sense of connection with who I am and what I have. If it has changed my life it can change it for you too. Spend twenty minutes every day, thinking of the good things you have done in your past and being grateful to people who inspired you and thanking the Lord for having given you this life. Thank your parents for the wealth of wisdom they have given you, and the love they showered you with.

"I cried because I had no shoes until I saw a man with who had no feet". This is so beautifully said. No matter how badly off you are, there are plenty of people who are suffering more than you are. Go to the slums of India and witness their living conditions, see the atrocities being inflicted on children in certain countries, hear the cries of women been forced into adultery, feel the pain of laborers working in adverse weather conditions and you will realize your life is much better and fuller in all aspects. Your difficulties do not make you weak. Your reactions to your difficulties make you weak. Your consequence depends on your focus during these tim Focus on your strengths to make them your only realty. If you focus on your weakness, they would be manifested all the more The choice, finally, is always yours.

What Are You Planting?

Don't be discouraged. It's often the last key in the bunch that opens the lock.

–Author Unknown

There is a difference in how the fern and the bamboo tree grow. Once you sow the seeds of both these plants and water them, you notice a rather startling difference. The fern will grow quite early and within one year, will reach its maximum height. But don't lose heart and keep on watering the bamboo seeds and fertilizing them regularly. It will take a lot of patience and even then you may not see a significant growth for a few more years. Somewhere in the fifth year, you will notice that within a span of six weeks the bamboo tree has grown quite tall – maybe a hundred feet while the fern is still two feet tall. The bamboo tree has shot up to a height which is way too impossible for the fern to achieve in its lifetime.

The bamboo tree takes time to grow but grows quite tall in the end. Growing a fern is, on the other hand, quite simple and there are immediate results but it does not grow consistently. At the end, the fern is quite small as compared to the bamboo tree. The ingredients of success are

Be careful of the Thoughts and Actions you sow

perseverance, patience and hard work. Every human achievement involves the rigorous working and waiting for results. Every Nobel laureate puts in years and years of effort and labour and every successful sportsman trains in a backbreaking manner for five years to get that Olympic gold. And what about every president of America? They go through the rather long and strenuous presidential campaign to realize their dreams. Every human achievement has been carefully crafted with the bricks of human sweat, sacrifices, patience, failures, breakdowns and moments of loss and only then were monumental goals realized.

There are lots of young girls and boys studying in school, colleges and institutes, there are people who are working and there are businessmen. They all have their own aspirations. All of them are carrying on with the hope one day they would be able to live life the way they want to. They find it difficult to move from the wrong job to the one they want to do, or sign up for a course they have wanted to do for a long time. They only wanted the fern at some point of time in their lives. They know they are made for better things but they are still in the hope of meager returns. Believing in quick fixes is no solution. It becomes a vicious cycle eventually. They're not quite sure of what they want from life. Their values are contradictory. I remember a time when I asked one of my friends why they went to work. And he just said he wanted to do something – that was all. So I asked him why. He said he needed to earn money to sustain himself. And I asked him why he needed to eat at all. 'To go to work the next day', he said. Poor chap works to earn and earns to work. He is stuck in a vicious circle of insignificance.

Let me ask you a question – If there is someone who is suffering from a deadly disease, and the doctor keeps on treating the symptoms, do you believe the disease will vanish? Would the person ever get better? You may treat blood pressure by having medicines and tranquilizers but if you continue with your lifestyle, how will the base cause ever be addressed? The problem will resurface very soon, and maybe with greater impact. So it is the same with life's quick fixes. So after some time, the problems will resurface with greater emphasis.

Look around you. You might find many people stuck in a situation called stuck-in-a-wrong-profession. SIWP in short. They might resort to more dangerous snares of temporary relief – they take marijuana, cocaine, heroin and all kinds of drugs to cure their symptoms. They go to beer bars, sit in cafés and try to get a taste of the freedom, comfort, ecstasy and passion which they always wanted every moment which they don't get at all.

Now I don't say that all these things are bad, I only say that these things should be our choices and not our necessities. We should be in control of our desires and not let them control our bodies and mind. The people who have made them their necessities in life will need the courage to grow a bamboo tree for themselves instead of growing just a fern. It is the same formula we need here – perseverance, patience and hard work. It releases them from the meaninglessness of insignificant work.

But some people do dare to leave their meaningless jobs for their coveted career, or start a business with an idea they believe in. They challenge conventions and develop new products. They change the lives of millions of people with the way they think. They laugh at failures, take a stand for the right cause and start revolutions.

The list of people who waited patiently for the bamboo to grow is quite long, and include names as illustrious as Abraham Lincoln, Nelson Mandela, Mahatma Gandhi, Martin Luther King Jr, Mother Teresa, Donald Trump, JK Rowling, Napoleon Hill, Angelina Jolie, Barack Obama, Deepak Chopra, Walt Disney, Steve Jobs, Oprah Winfrey and Bill Gates. And I firmly believe you can also grow that bamboo tree in this one lifetime gifted specially to you if you are guided by your own inner compass.

But did it take six weeks or five years for the bamboo to grow? The people who dared to cultivate the bamboo tree knew that at any point of time if they stopped watering and fertilizing the bamboo seeds in these five years the monumental outcome will not be realized. Their patient labours realized their dreams and the bamboo grew to a gigantic ninety feet.

The Skill/Will Dilemma

There is no chance, no destiny, no fate that can circumvent or hinder or control the firm resolve of a determined soul.

–Ella Wheeler Wilcox

People who are still living in the darkness of their meaningless life and who are imprisoned by the shackles of limited thinking perhaps don't know how to start afresh. They believe they don't have the skills to start something new or to move to a new profession. Their past life holds them back. They can never believe in themselves. They assume that their current capabilities are not developed enough to begin a new life. That is just a myth.

Your WILL can make mountains move

Skill and will are the two things that really make a difference as far as success is concerned. One may be an expert in doing his/her work, doing it efficiently and right the first time itself. He may also have done this task earlier so many times that he has attained a superiority that others can only hope for. He has, therefore, successfully developed a skill. If one has a certain skill, he is bound to be successful in that task. A dancer can never be a successful salesperson and a communications expert will never be able to prepare a proper accounting report. Your skill will only be effective in the right situation. A person's will has something more to offer. One can use his will in any situation, unlike one's skill. Your willpower is directly connected with the strain of internal motivation running within you. When you have a desire to do a task and you are not forced into doing it, you are driven by your will. When you have a desire, you internal motivation is at work. It tells your will to go the extra mile and create a difference.

But can we say which is the more important ingredient? I shall tell you the story of Robert, who was very good at developing softwares but didn't want to learn software coding. He stuck to the job because he needed to do something. And there was his colleague who was very good with softwares but had the perseverance and willingness to learn all about it. So he started with a small project and quickly began to learn more about tools and strategies to develop software modules. He started with the small modules and gradually went ahead to learn the more difficult ones. He had the spirit to learn and hence developed the same competence as had been possessed by Robert

But the story did not end here; this person went further and began coding innovatively using more advance tools. He didn't limit himself to his job responsibilities but consistently went beyond his job description to do things to satisfy his internal drive. Where there is a will, there is a way.

The will exerts a powerful force on a person's ability to use and sharpen his skills. In the above case, Robert had a standard set of skills, which was quite acceptable for his job but his friend went way ahead of him when he tried to acquire a new set of skills. You can, if you allow it, your "Will" is going to:

Take you far ahead of your original potential
Stretch you to your utmost limits
Drive you ahead of your failures
Give you more emotional strength
Help you grow from within
Change every aspect of your life for the better
Help you learn new skills and, finally, take you to the heights you deserve

If you have the will to do something without having the required skill, you can be trained into possessing the skill. But without the will you will never get a task done, you will never be successful enough to be numbered among the best in your profession. It is really the will you need more than skill. Success depends completely on how motivated you are. The result will depend primarily on your willpower.

Your will also denotes your self-control. Will is your self-control. It also influences the amount of restraint with which you conduct yourself. A study was conducted by psychologist Walter Mischel, which was also called the Marshmallow Test. This test was administered on four-year olds to exhibit delayed gratification – a measure of the amount of self-control children have over themselves. The children were brought into a room where delicious marshmallows were kept in front of them, on a table. Scientists told the children they could either have the marshmallow or wait for fifteen minutes and they would get two treats. Some ate at once and some of them delayed their gratification.

The scientists kept a watch on the children and found out that the ones with more restraint grew up to be better-behaved, well-read and were also less prone to any kind of addiction. Willpower helps you in every aspect of your life. It is willpower that makes people recover from terminal illness, it's willpower which inspires people to hit back after they've hit an all-time low and it is willpower, again, which inspires a rags-to-riches story. Developing willpower is just like developing a muscle: you need to exercise your willpower in different situations and the stronger it will get. All the changes need not be made within one day. Work on it gradually and one fine day, you will find you have created a better life for yourself

Faith and Reasons

> *Faith is knowledge within the heart, beyond the reach of proof.*
>
> –Kahlil Gibran

Possibilities and impossibilities are creations of the mind. What appears impossible to someone might be easy for someone else. When some countries assumed that it was impossible to go to the moon, there were some others who actually did it! Soon after, other countries followed. In 1954, Roger Bannister broke the one minute mile barrier for the first time in human history. For years people believed it was impossible to run a mile in less than a minute, yet Roger Bannister broke the record. In the year that followed, many others were able to break the one-minute mile barrier.

Have enough faith and enough reasons for your faith

I had no idea other people influenced us so much. We are actually influenced by seeing impossible ideas being realized around us. But what do young minds think of such possibilities? What did Roger Bannister think before he broke the record? What did the scientists of the nation think, when they were the first ones to reach the moon? What fuelled these ideas and these people? Faith. Sir Martin Luther King, Jr. said "Faith is taking the first step even when you don't see the whole staircase." You may not be able to see the complete path at once but trust yourself and take a step forward.

When we travel, can we see the entire path at once? Do we see the miles we are to walk while we are setting out? We see the roads as we travel. We experience our journey while we are on our way. We do not need to know the way our destination will look when we start travelling. You don't have to see what you are going to achieve, just take one step at a time and the road to the impossible will light up.

Faith is fathered by reasons. Reasons make it possible to do the impossible. Reasons give the power to individuals to have unflinching faith. Reasons create a meaning when there is no meaning in life. Reasons launch people from mediocrity to excellence. Reasons inspire a group of individuals to give their lives for a nation. Reasons move individuals to do the impossible for their loved ones. Terminally-ill patients survive for a reason. A worthy reason has the power to transform someone's life.

"I have got a reason and now I will live" could be how a seventy-year old man (suffering from diabetes and other diseases) reacts when he sees his newborn grandchild. The old man found a reason to stretch himself beyond the zone of possibilities. It has been seven years and he is having a lovely family life with his grandson. Another man said, "I have diabetes and I will die because I have nothing left to live for" and surely he died soon. The death was an outcome chosen by the old man by not finding a reason compelling enough to live for and make a conscious effort. You can't search for reasons; you must create them within yourself.

With emotionally-compelling reasons you can unleash your true potential. Find out the big 'why' in your life. It can change your attitude towards life altogether. Search for the reasons behind a challenge you might be facing. If, for example, a girl wants to reduce her weight but she isn't motivated enough, she can ask herself why she would like to reduce weight. She created compelling reasons for herself. She told herself she could have more energy and vitality, she could fit into her old clothes, she could attract a lovely person, she can develop more self-esteem at work.

The more reasons you have the more energy you can generate. For a few people only one reason is more than enough to initiate action while others need more reasons to start working. Every person acts because he has reasons to do so, and if there are many reasons, chances of the reasons being acted upon increase. Human beings are emotional, and if we can give ourselves enough emotional reason to act, we would progress better. Doctors who handle clinically-depressed and suicidal people delve deeper into the patients' lives in order to find a reason for them to live happily. The doctors know how important it is for them to find a reason for these people to live.

If you wish to harness your potential, have enough compelling reasons to:

- smile
- believe
- create joy
- love
- work hard
- live your passion

One of my friends wanted to be in a relationship but couldn't take out time to spend developing a relationship. But he wanted a relationship for himself. He asked himself why he wants a relationship in the first place. When you pen down your reasons on a paper, you can see a big list. In the mind the reasons are scattered, so a good strategy is to pen it down on paper. Those reasons may be too confusing within your mind so writing them down would be a good idea. Faith comes from reasons. Have reasons, have faith and no one can stop you from doing the impossible.

What's in this for me?

1. Live for a worthier cause than earning money.
   'Create a legacy'

2. Appreciate the wealth of experience you have gathered.
   'Be thankful for what you have
   and you shall have more'

3. As you sow, so shall you reap.
   'Plant good seeds for
   a better future'

4. Your willpower can move you and others to greatness.
   'If you have the will, you will
   acquire the skill'

5. Faith and reasons can create power.
   'Have compelling enough reasons
   to get to your destination'

Acknowledgements

I will thank my family for supporting me throughout the journey of writing my book and encouraging me to live my dreams – my mother Ms Mini Lal, father Dr Ajay Kumar Lal, my cute little sister, Kiku and my masi, Ms Suman Nalwa. I thank my friends and associates for believing in me and my work.

I would thank Jaico Publications for their effort during the journey for helping me reach out to people across the country. Special thanks to Srija, Sandhya and Akash for making one of my dreams come true. You have done a great service. Thank you.

Lastly, I would like to thank all the people who had said "You can't do it" and the ones who had put me down several times, only to see me coming up again. You gave me power.

Thank you.

About the Author

NISHIT LAL, after a brief stint with IT giant Infosys, found his passion in helping people live better lives. He is a performance consultant, who helps people break through their imaginary barriers, amplify their performances and achieve tangible results in their business and personal lives.

He conducts leadership and emotional intelligence workshops for a wide range of audiences using Neuro Linguistic Programming techniques. Backed by professional degrees in technology and human resources management, he conducts entertaining, yet powerful training programs, which help people gain momentum and instantly make changes to their lives.

He is an active writer and has authored two books in the past.

Nishit Lal can be reached at: nishitlal@outlook.com

JAICO PUBLISHING HOUSE

Elevate Your Life. Transform Your World.

ESTABLISHED IN 1946, Jaico Publishing House is home to world-transforming authors such as Sri Sri Paramahansa Yogananda, Osho, The Dalai Lama, Sri Sri Ravi Shankar, Robin Sharma, Deepak Chopra, Jack Canfield, Eknath Easwaran, Devdutt Pattanaik, Khushwant Singh, John Maxwell, Brian Tracy and Stephen Hawking.

Our late founder Mr. Jaman Shah first established Jaico as a book distribution company. Sensing that independence was around the corner, he aptly named his company Jaico ('Jai' means victory in Hindi). In order to service the significant demand for affordable books in a developing nation, Mr. Shah initiated Jaico's own publications. Jaico was India's first publisher of paperback books in the English language.

While self-help, religion and philosophy, mind/body/spirit, and business titles form the cornerstone of our non-fiction list, we publish an exciting range of travel, current affairs, biography, and popular science books as well. Our renewed focus on popular fiction is evident in our new titles by a host of fresh young talent from India and abroad. Jaico's recently established Translations Division translates selected English content into nine regional languages.

Jaico's Higher Education Division (HED) is recognized for its student-friendly textbooks in Business Management and Engineering which are in use countrywide.

In addition to being a publisher and distributor of its own titles, Jaico is a major national distributor of books of leading international and Indian publishers. With its headquarters in Mumbai, Jaico has branches and sales offices in Ahmedabad, Bangalore, Bhopal, Bhubaneswar, Chennai, Delhi, Hyderabad, Kolkata and Lucknow.

SINCE 1946